UNLOCKING HEAVEN'S POWER

UNLOCKING HEAVEN'S POWER

JOHN PAUL JACKSON

Foreword by Marcus and Joni Lamb

Unlocking Heaven's Power
John Paul Jackson. Copyright ©2015 Streams Ministries International.

Published by Daystar Television Network under license from Streams Ministries International.

Produced with assistance from Creative Enterprises Studio, premier publishing services group of Books, Bach & Beyond, Inc., Bedford, TX. CreativeEnterprisesStudio.com

Unless otherwise noted, Scripture quotations are from the New King James Version (NKJV®), copyright 1979, 1980, 1982, Thomas Nelson, Inc., Publishers. Used by permission.

Quotations designated ESV are from THE ENGLISH STANDARD TRANSLATION. © 2001 by The American Bible Society. Used by permission. All rights reserved.

Quotations designated NCV are from the New Century Version®. Copyright © 1987, 1988, 1991 by Thomas Nelson, Inc. All rights reserved.

Quotations designated NIV are from The Holy Bible, New International Version. Copyright © 1973, 1978, 1984, 2011, International Bible Society. Used by permission of Zondervan Bible Publishers.

ISBN: 978-0-9910409-0-2

Printed in the United States of America

15 16 17 18 19 20 LS 6 5 4 3 2 1

Contents

Contents

FOREWORD

Dear Partners,

So many of you loved John Paul Jackson, and he was a great friend to Daystar. Recently, he was promoted to Heaven, but he has forever left an indelible mark on our hearts with his teaching and wisdom. Through his time here on earth, he wrote the following words of wisdom that we believe he received straight from the throne of God.

We were blessed to have access to this incredible manuscript. *Unlocking Heaven's Power*, one of John Paul's previously unpublished works, and we are making this wonderful book available to our partners.

In these next few pages, you'll read step-by-step instructions for every believer to access the full power of Heaven. John Paul explains how to maximize Heaven's help in the world we live in today, whether you have just begun this journey or you are seasoned in your walk with Christ.

Taking the basics that every Believer should know, John Paul lays them out in a simple yet profound newness that is both refreshing and applicable. You can make it a quick read and gain insight or slowly relish each chapter, meditating on the scriptures and contemplations he shares. And as you dive into these pages, we know this book will be of great benefit in guiding you to overcome the daily struggles we as Christians face.

To John Paul, we'd like to say that we miss you, but we are grateful you left behind such anointed writings. Thanks to your work, our lives are still being impacted through the ever-loving Savior you so passionately served.

MARCUS AND JONI LAMB
Founders, Daystar Television Network

Introduction

A river at flood stage has very few boundaries. It is powerful. It can demolish structures that have stood for centuries and rearrange the surface of the earth. It is very difficult to restrain a wild current once it has tasted freedom. This is a book about reaching the place where God is unrestrained in your life. When God is unrestrained, everything changes.

I would love for God to be as unrestrained in my life as a river at flood stage. I don't want Him to have to endure boundaries with me—"fences" I erect out of ignorance, fear, or sin. I know He will answer this desire, for it began as His desire. I am simply asking Him for what He has already placed in my heart. He doesn't want there to be walls between us either. He wants to be able to reveal Himself through me unhindered to the world—without a veil, without shadows or restrictions.

The "fences" we have with God aren't necessarily easy to find. They aren't covered with flashing lights and bright warning colors, so we can see them from a distance and remove them. Many things can hold us back in the process of following God, and we don't necessarily realize what's happening. Instead, we just know we have questions:

- *Why do the same things seem to happen to me over and over again?*

- *Why do I sometimes feel like I'm not even saved?*

- *Why do I feel like I am hanging on by the skin of my teeth, finger-nails digging into the edge of the cliff? If the ground moves at all, I am done for!*

- *Can my life improve, or will it just always be this way?*

Early in my walk with God, I asked that last question a lot. Far too often I would look at my life and think, *When are things going to change? It seems like it's been this way forever!* I have learned that whenever we ask that question over and over, we are in a cycle. God has taken us around the mountain, but why? We have come right back to the same starting point. It may be with a different person, but it is the same issue. It may be with a different pastor, but it is the same issue. It may be with different events, but it is the same issue. A thousand things can make us angry, for example, and if God is working on our anger problem, He may use all thousand to get our attention. We find ourselves in the same sort of situation all over again, and we end up right where we were before. Anytime we have cycles in our lives, it is because we haven't dealt with the issue God wants to deal with inside of us.

Why does this keep happening to me?

When are things going to change?

Another common question is, *Why do my unsaved friends seem to be doing better than I am?* Or, *Why does it seem that the greedy and selfish are rewarded in life?* The prophet Jeremiah asked a similar question: "Why does the way of the wicked prosper?" (Jeremiah 12:1). The ancient psalmists talked about envying those who didn't know the Lord and seeing the triumph and prosperity of the wicked (Psalms 73:3; 94:3). Why is it that life often seems difficult for the children of God?

Will my children have the same problems I have?

That is the question that brings it home the most. It is one thing to ask, "Why does everything happen to me?" But it is a much different matter to ask, "Will this happen to my children as well?" As parents, if our children are sick we would rather be sick. We want to bear their pain for them. We would take their place if given the option. That is what parents do. Will our actions and choices now affect our children? Yes, they will. If we don't change our ways, our children will have the same issues we have.

There are "fences" we need to pull down—for the sake of our children, for the sake of the legacy we leave behind. Our children seldom see beyond the fences we erect. I want to deal with the issues in my life so my children don't have to deal with them. We can change for the sake of our children.

A lot of us don't think of it that way. We personalize it only, and we don't look at the ripple effect on the generations, which is why Scripture says that curses can be passed on to the third and fourth generations and, in some cases, even ten generations. We don't think of the ongoing consequences and impact of our actions, generation after generation after generation.

Each of these questions can be answered in one word: *choices.* Choices are important because they comprise your thoughts. Every choice you make starts with a thought.

So what are you thinking?

It is all too easy to become alienated from what true life in God should be like (Ephesians 4:24). Giving to the church does not make all our thought processes godly; just because we pray before meals or gave our hearts to Jesus as children does not mean every thought we think is aligned with His Word. God wants to stop anything that hinders His purpose in our lives, including our decision-making skills and the thoughts that drive those skills. He wants to reveal His power on our behalf. He wants to do things for us that we couldn't even imagine. He is an active God. A powerful God. A God who is not limited by tradition or church culture. Only in respect to our belief systems is He limited. Why? Because it is hard for us to give God permission to do something that we don't believe He can or wants to do.

Too many of us just don't really believe in our hearts that He will come through for us. We might believe in our minds, in our intellect, but we don't really believe in our hearts. We aren't in a place where we believe He will be an adversary to our adversaries and an enemy to our enemies. We don't really believe that His purpose in us will not be stopped. We don't really believe that He will send angels to aid us in accomplishing His purpose for us.

Yet there is a way of life in God that is far superior to the way we have lived up to this point. Salvation is just the *entrance*; it is the threshold to a fantastic life, not just an event that took place in the past.

Hopefully, this book will take that understanding from our heads to our hearts, where we can believe it on a daily basis. When we truly believe it, our response to difficulty changes in dramatic ways. We begin to see life as the adventure God made it to be, and the enemy flees.

Digesting and understanding the precepts written in this book will help you create the spiritual atmosphere that will justify all Heaven's beings acting on your behalf. In addition, you will understand more of God's ways and recognize His activity in your life on a daily basis.

— JOHN PAUL JACKSON

Chapter 1

THE POWER OF CHOICE

Setting Yourself Up for Heaven's Help

When I was twenty-six years old, I took a car ride with one of my best friends. This was before I entered ministry; my wife and I had just gotten married, and my friend was a doctor who was known to be gifted and insightful.

He told me, "John Paul, you have so much ability, but you are not using it. Until you change the way you think, you are going to languish, just as you are languishing now."

I got upset. *Who does he think he is? Just because he's my friend does not give him the right to tell me that. He just doesn't know my life! He doesn't know what I've gone through. He doesn't know what I've had to overcome. He doesn't know anything about me. I've known him for about nine or ten months, and until this moment I really liked the guy. Boy, this is not right!*

Now that I am older, and hopefully wiser, I realize how right my friend was. Had I changed my thinking when I was twenty-six, my life would have been radically different. At the time, I assumed my perceptions were truth. I thought my worldview was reality, when it was actually reality only to me. It was not reality to anyone else, yet I used it to make choices. The problem is that false reality results in false choices—that is, *wrong* choices, and wrong choices give you wrong results.

Over and over again, I wondered, *Why does such-and-such keep happening to me?*

Finally, the Lord took pity on me and answered, "Because you keep making the same choice! If you would change your choice, you would change your results."

Really? I was surprised. *Oh.*

So I began changing my choices. I remember saying to myself, *I'm going to change the choice I usually make in this situation because I keep getting a bad result. I'm not going to do what I always do.* Keep in mind, I was still thoroughly convinced that what I normally did was the correct response—but I decided to try a different response instead. Needless to say, I was surprised when the new choice ended up being the better choice, and for the first time I achieved a different result! A better result.

One thing led to another. I began to make a lot of changes and recognize the various ruts I was in. *I'm going to keep making different choices,* I thought.

Many of us are familiar with Proverbs 23:7, but we don't always stop to consider it at depth. What is the outcome of thinking with the heart?

TRY A NEW WAY

As he thinks in his heart, so is he.

— Proverbs 23:7

Why "are" we what we think in our hearts? And more importantly, if thinking in the heart is so important—*what are we thinking?*

As Proverbs 23:7 says, we become what we think in our hearts. A man who thinks he is a good man will *become* a better man. A woman who thinks she is a good mother will become a better mother. Conversely, a doctor who thinks he is worthless will have a difficult time accomplishing great things. A woman who believes she is a poor executive will struggle in her field.

If we don't understand how our thoughts govern our choices and everything that follows, we won't be able to change. We will stay here—we will remain right where and what we are today. Five years from now, our lives will look the same. We will build a cycle that will be very difficult to break because we think we belong in that cycle. We *become* that cycle.

- Every success or failure begins with an action.

- Every action begins with a choice.

- Every choice begins with a thought.

- Every thought begins with an attitude.

Whether we know it or not, the end result is that we are a product of the choices we have made. Our thinking created a pathway to our success or failure. Years ago, we chose to be where we are right now. We made the decision with our thoughts, and every choice has consequences, expected or unexpected. We are where we are today because of choices like where we went to school, whom we married, if we had children, if we didn't have children, the job we took, the house we live in, the car we drive, and so on. And all these choices came about because of how we were thinking at the time.

Outside influences are not responsible for where we are mentally, physically, spiritually, emotionally, and financially. We can't blame our spouse for where we are today—because we made those choices. I don't know how many times I have counseled men and women who told me, "My spouse is holding me back!"

Wives say, "If my husband would just do such and such, I could walk into what God created me to do!" Husbands say the same thing: "If my wife would just do this, I could walk into what God created me to do!"

But that just isn't true. These are excuses because we make our own choices! I have found that in many situations, it is *my* actions that compel my wife to do what she does. My actions provoke her and propel her thoughts in a certain direction. So if I change my actions, my wife's thinking changes. It is not that I am somehow controlling her; I am showing her that she can trust me, which causes her thinking to change. If I want to achieve a different result, I need to change the choice I am making in the moment. At the time, I thought the right choice would be to react a certain way, when that was the *wrong* choice. The right choice was to respond in a different way—and not react at all.

Every decision is made with a choice, and every choice begins with a thought. Therefore, it is of the utmost importance that we learn to guard our thoughts. When we guard our thoughts, we can think the right thoughts and make the right choices from those right thoughts. How? That is what this book is about. When we blame outside forces (individuals, economic issues, the college we chose, the teachers we had, or whatever else), we remain caught in the web of our past. Blame shifting acts like flypaper—once it snags us, we can't get away from it. We remain right where we are, going through the same situations over and over.

The past will always recur. Until we change our thinking.

STEPS TO YOUR DESTINY IN GOD

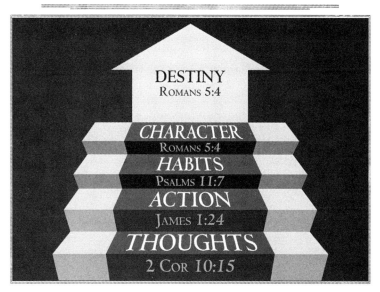

Commit your works to the LORD, and
your thoughts will be established.

— Proverbs 23:7

Committing our works to the Lord is an attitude about who God is—specifically, who He is for us. If you are a deist who believes that God created the world and then left us to fend for ourselves, you are going to approach life a lot differently than a person who believes that God is intricately involved in his or her everyday activities.

And God is intricately involved. We have no idea how much attention He gives each of us. He set up a system in Heaven that includes spiritual beings—creatures that can move on our behalf to help us reach the purposes for which our Father created us. He created angels to help us accomplish the very thing we need accomplished in our lives. One-third of the angels fell (Revelation 12:4), but that leaves two-thirds still in God's service, which means the odds are two to one on our behalf.

You could think about it like this: Even if God weren't omni-present and all-powerful, the odds are still with us. However, since He is all-powerful, there are no odds—it is going to happen, if we trust Him and believe His Word.

CONTEMPLATIONS

Your thinking creates a pathway to success or failure.
When you think about your future, what holds your attention
the most?

Is that thing negative or positive?
Do you walk away feeling hopeful or depressed?

Every choice begins with a thought.
Can you connect a significant life decision to a
particular thought
you had on a regular basis?

Chapter 2

ADVERSITY: THE UNEXPECTED TWIST

How God Uses Difficult Times to Prepare His People

Greatness is a gentleman, which is somewhat unfortunate. If greatness were not a gentleman, we would become great whether we wanted to or not. Greatness would seize us with violence. It wouldn't be up to us—our will wouldn't play a significant role, and neither would our faithfulness, personal choices, and perseverance.

Instead, greatness is birthed through hardship and testing. It arises choice by choice. We bleed. We sweat. We fall down. We get up and try again. Sometimes it feels like we are living in the dark, because we can no longer see the road. We don't know what to expect. We can keep going, believing in faith, or we can turn back, listening to our fears. Greatness comes as we make the choice to look at our Father in faith and not give in to fear and doubt.

Oddly enough, fear and faith share the same basic root: both are the belief that something is going to happen. Faith is the belief that something good is going to happen, while fear is the belief that something bad is going to happen. Fear says, "Greater is the enemy's ability to pummel me than God's ability to preserve me." When we believe the enemy is stronger than God, we throw open the doors of our circumstances and give the enemy the right to attack us. Fear is not wisdom. It is an invitation to the enemy.

Fear does not know the Father's heart. When we fear, we are declaring with our thoughts and actions, "I cannot trust God to take care of me. I do not expect God to save me. I expect the enemy to gain the victory in my life." Though fear and faith share the same basic root, greatness and fear are strangers to one another. It isn't that somewhere in this journey to greatness, we somehow lose the ability to fear or that we cease to feel afraid—it is that true greatness is married to faith in God, and faith in God always takes the road less traveled, despite the risk involved. Faith looks at the screaming winds, the waves, the dark skies, the water swamping the boat, and asks, "What are these things coming against me? They are nothing! No matter what tries to drown me, I know the Lord will overcome it. Let's do this together, God. Let's see what You got."

That is the beginning of greatness.

THE POWER OF FAITH IN GOD

But Jesus looked at them and said to them, "With men
this is impossible, but with God all things are possible."

— Matthew 19:26

Faith is not what we expect it to be. It exists and thrives in the realm of the unseen; therefore, by definition, it cannot be something predictable. It is not "human." It is not built within our own power. Nothing about it resembles human strength or human means. It is wild. It is outside our boundaries. It is extravagant.

Why? Because God is all of those things.

Faith looks like God, and it behaves in a way that is true of His Holy Spirit. Jesus looked at water and saw how it could be a bridge. He looked at the tomb of a dead man and saw them eating dinner together that night. Faith supersedes the circumstances of life and the physical laws of the world, and it allows us to take actions that are completely outside the human paradigm. Man cannot walk across the surface of a sea. The sea is not a bridge—but nothing is impossible with God. All of us have read Matthew 19:26, but few of us know how to live like it is true!

I want to be like Peter in Matthew 14. On the Sea of Galilee, he took a good look at his circumstances. He saw the storm, the waves, and his companions trying to keep afloat. He felt the force of the wind and the pounding of his own heart, and he did not come to a human decision—a decision that took into account the paradigms of man. Instead, he brought his hand to his mouth and shouted across the water to Jesus, who was pretending He was on some type of unseen bridge.

"This would be a lot more interesting if it were a little more difficult!" Peter cried. "If You can do this, I want to do this too! Invite me on the water with You. Let's do this together" (John Paul paraphrase).

In another story, in a different storm, Jesus looked at the disciples as they cowered in terror and asked them, "Why are you afraid, O you of little faith?" He then spoke to the tempest and calmed it as He would a child. "Peace. Be still."

When God chooses to kill fear in us, He does not *remove* the things we are afraid of. Instead, He does something unexpected and unpredictable that is outside human logic—He takes us *deeper* into the very thing we fear. He uses adversity to prepare us for greatness.

One time when I was complaining to the Lord, I said, "Why are You taking us through so many storms? Why? Why are You allowing this to happen to me?"

He replied, "Will you stop complaining? All you want is little-bitty battles!"

"Yes, that's right, Lord!" I said. "I'm tired of big battles. I want little-bitty battles!"

"But, son, little-bitty battles produce little-bitty victories and make little-bitty men. What have you asked Me to do for you?"

"To make me a great man of God!" I said. "But does it *have* to be great battles?"

He answered, "Great battles produce great victories, which produce great men of God. Champions are made because they have fought great battles to obtain great victories to become great champions. Now, which do you want?"

I weakly replied, "I want little-bitty battles and to become a champion!"

And the Lord softly answered, "Well, it doesn't work that way. What do you want?"

I say the same thing to you as He said to me—what do you want? Do you want to become a champion of the Most High? If you do, it might be time to stop running from your problems. Instead, let God keep you alive. Stay in the storm, and let God bail you out. Exercise courage, and watch the miracle take place. If He told you to do something, it is *His* responsibility to keep you afloat, and He will do it.

Are we usurping God's authority by taking matters into our own hands, instead of waiting and letting Him take care of it? We say we trust God, but as fast as we can, we try to change our circumstances, apparently forgetting how God says in Proverbs 21:1 that the heart of a king is like a river and He turns it wherever He wants it to go. What if it is our hearts that need changing and we're simply telling Him, "Back off, God, and let me do it"?

Adversity is the beginning of greatness, and we need to accept the preparations God allows to come. Among other advantages, they tell us where and how our thinking needs to change.

No matter what we face, 1 Thessalonians 5:18 remains a true reality for us: "In everything give thanks, for this is the will of God in Christ Jesus for you."

The will of God does not mean He likes it. We often confuse *will* with *pleasure*, so we end up reading the verse like this: "In everything give thanks, for this is the pleasure of God in Christ Jesus for you." That line of thinking becomes problematic because the next step is assuming that whenever the enemy attacks us, it makes God happy. *If something bad happens to me and it's the "will of God" concerning me, that must mean that God wanted it to happen. It must mean that God takes pleasure in the bad thing happening to me. Is God sadistic? How could that be, God?*

But 1 Thessalonians 5:18 is not talking about God's pleasure; it is talking about His will. There is a dramatic difference! Scripture tells us that God values His word above His name (Psalm 138:2). His Word lays out His divine order, which can be summed up this way:

> The closer you are to God, the less room evil has to operate in your life; conversely the further you are from God, the more room evil has to operate in the events around you.

God does not take pleasure in our pain. He doesn't take pleasure in Satan winning anything in our lives. He *does* take pleasure in the fact that justice can be rendered when we give ourselves totally to Him. He loves being justified in taking action on our behalf. He takes pleasure in His will coming to pass and in bringing people closer to Him.

The pleasure of God should never be confused with the will of God. Essentially, His will states, "I have established a judicial process, and in My judicial process, I cannot legislate that people love Me. I *want* them to love Me, but I cannot *make* them love Me. Therefore, My judicial process not only allows them to get closer to Me, but it also allows Me to do great things on their behalf. In order for Satan not to say that I, God, am unjust, I must make this equal in every aspect. My justice must be balanced. Satan feels like he can capture the world through the knowledge of good and evil (the soul), but I know that My Spirit will win. I will capture the world through My Spirit."

It is imperative that we distinguish between God's will and God's pleasure. If William crashes his motorcycle and breaks his leg, it does not give God pleasure. At the same time, He might be teaching William that he takes too many risks with his motorcycle. God could be saying, "This is what happens when you take this type of risk." It is His will, not His pleasure, that says, "I will let you know the consequence for your action, so you can change the action and therefore the consequence." The issue is not the motorcycle itself; it is the attitude of risk-taking. It is not the pleasure of God that allows William to suffer a painful consequence; it is His will, which understands the benefits of maturity. Thus the reason for the chastening of the Lord, who chastens all He loves (Hebrews 12:6).

TESTS OF THE LORD

I, the LORD, search the heart; I test the mind.

— Jeremiah 17:10

An important thing to understand is that we experience certain events and situations simply because God is testing our hearts to see if we really love Him and are impassioned for Him. We also go through many things because God is testing our minds to see if they have been renewed to the degree that we respond the way He would respond. As God, He already knows how we will respond—but He allows us the opportunity to use as we see fit the gifts and abilities He gives us. He tests our minds to see how we will handle His gifts, and adversity is one of these tests.

A plethora of things need to be considered in order for God to have the fullest and most consistent manifestation of power on the earth. We need to learn to position ourselves to maximize Heaven's help.

CONTEMPLATIONS

Adversity is preparation for greatness.
How do you usually respond to adversity?

Accept the adversity, or "preparations,"
God allows to come your way,
because adversity can tell you
where your thinking needs to change.
Do you look at adversity as an obstacle or opportunity?

In everything give thanks;
for this is the will of God in Christ Jesus for you.
— I THESSALONIANS 5:18

Chapter 3

The Mind Game

Setting Your Mind on Things Above

Unlocking Heaven's power can be boiled down to one basic question: what is your focus?

In a broad, general sense, there are only two possible answers to that question: you will be empire focused or Kingdom focused.

An empire, or earthly, mentality says, "Everything is about me." In a ministry setting, it is a narcissistic point of view that builds its own world before helping you with yours: "I want you to help me. You want to help me. Therefore, come help me, and I'll get to do what I want to do. If you have anything you want to do, maybe after I get what I want, I'll help you get what you want."

In a church setting, an empire focus does not accept the possibility that God would move in a different church. If the church across the street experiences a move of God in which the Holy Spirit is showing up and healing people, an empire mentality looks at the situation and starts shaking its head. "That cannot be God, because if it *were* God, it would be happening here."

As long as we are empire minded, we limit our world to being only as big as we are. Our weaknesses hinder our work, and eventually we find that our positive attributes aren't great enough to overcome all of our weaknesses.

God intentionally created us to need the gifts and input of other people, and a Kingdom mind-set recognizes this quickly. It is a recognition that breeds humility and perceives God's design: "I will never accomplish what I am created to accomplish without the help of others. I need other people." A Kingdom mind-set also releases the assets of Heaven. In many cases, we receive the help of God's angels and His Holy Spirit when we are helping others. So in the course of serving others, our own needs are met, even if we don't recognize it at the time, because God has sent unseen help.

The book of Colossians shows us what Kingdom and empire mentalities can look like. Right off the bat, the apostle Paul stated in chapter 2 that God wants to give us something, but someone is trying to keep us from getting it. "Let no one cheat you of your reward," he said. In other words, something is trying to keep you from what God wants you to have—how are you going to work with God to see His intended outcome in your life?

The "new man" is renewed in wisdom and spiritual knowledge according to the image of Him who created him (Colossians 3:10). God created us according to His own image—we are supposed to look like God in our thoughts, which then leads us to look like Him through our choices and actions. People should look at us and start to think, *Wow. I see the presence of God on that person.*

When people look at us, do they categorize us with their unsaved friends? Or do they look at us and start thinking about Jesus?

EVIDENCE OF EMPIRE THINKING: SELF-PROMOTION WITH SELF-EFFORT (COLOSSIANS 2:18–3:10)

As we read through Colossians 2:18–3:10, we often ignore the long inventory of "cautions" Paul gives, but these cautions are the initial list of things that hinder Heaven from acting on our behalf. This is the empire side of the equation. We are to "put off" these things, but unfortunately, some of us often overlook, ignore, or even self-justify any that we find in our lives:

- False humility: the desire for others to think we are something we are not

- Worship of angels: seeking the help of angels before we seek the help of God

- Vanity increasing from a fleshly (sensual, worldly) mind: using things of the material world to cover our spiritual flaws

- Appearance of wisdom but no value against flesh (doctrines of humanity; self-imposed religion; neglect of the body; "do not touch, taste, or handle"): thinking we can perfect ourselves to the place where God would accept us

- Fornication: sex outside of marriage

- Uncleanness: defilement; living in a state of unrighteousness before God

- Passion: uncontrolled emotional outbursts such as rage, bitterness, and unforgiveness

- Evil desires: seeking the destruction of another's physical body, reputation, property, or belongings

- Covetousness: idolatry; wanting something God gave to someone else to the point you obsess about having it or even despise the one who does

- Anger: failure to accept what God allowed to come your way

- Wrath: uncontrolled actions that destroy what God created (thinking you can act for God)

- Malice: vengeance (thinking you are justified in hurting another for what he or she did to you)

- Blasphemy: attributing the Holy Spirit's actions as being of Satan

- Filthy language: coarse jesting; lewd or sexually charged jokes or speech

- Lying: speaking falsehood to denigrate, deceive, or defame someone or something in opposition to the very fabric of the Holy Spirit of truth

At times these actions and activities could seem right or justifiable in some fashion, but they end up being vehicles to coerce people or even God, if possible, to do something for us. They are not things that allow God to act on our behalf. That is the point of this book—learning to live in such a way that God can do whatever He wants to do in our lives. We maximize Heaven's help by living the way God created us to live.

EVIDENCE OF KINGDOM THINKING: ACKNOWLEDGING GOD AND HIS WAYS ABOVE OUR OWN (COLOSSIANS 2:12–17)

Here is the Kingdom side of the equation. As we develop a Kingdom mind-set, these things become second nature to us:

- Renewed in knowledge: thinking according to the truth of God's Kingdom

- Tender mercies (Psalm 25:6)

- Kindness (Nehemiah 9:17)

- Humility (Matthew 11:29)

- Meekness (Philippians 2:8)

- Longsuffering (Numbers 14:18)

- Bearing with one another: comforting each other; helping support one another and find healing

- Forgiving one another (Ephesians 4:32)

- Putting on love: doing all things in love

- Letting the peace of God rule our hearts (Colossians 3:15; Philippians 4:17)

- Recognizing we are called to one body (Ephesians 4:4)

- Being thankful (Colossians 3:15)

- Letting the Word of Christ dwell in us, which washes us from all unrighteousness

- Teaching others: helping others to reach the purposes for which God created them

- Singing with grace: helping comfort, edify, and exhort others more than promoting our own gifts

How do we begin to transition our minds from an empire mentality to a Kingdom mentality? First, we need to believe that God actually wants to use us to advance His Kingdom. That is the first step. He places the seed of the Kingdom inside us, and we then have to conquer our internal world before we can be fully used to conquer the external world. This internal world is conquered as we transform our thinking from an empire mentality to a Kingdom mentality. Jesus said that it is the Father's good pleasure to give us the Kingdom (Luke 12:32). Having the things of the Kingdom is not just a good idea on our part, something we think we should possess—but God Himself wants us to have the things of the Kingdom. If we are convinced we can't succeed, we won't be able to succeed because our thinking is wrong. How could He act on our behalf if we believe He won't? He rarely acts on our behalf unless we truly believe He wants to do something for us.

We are tripartite beings, and every day we make choices that elevate the flesh, the soul, or the spirit. The result of our choices will be spiritual or earthly—and those choices will determine our destiny. When we pray, "Your Kingdom come; Your will be done, on earth as it is in heaven," we are asking God, "Change my mind-set! Change the mental strongholds that keep me from walking with You and from recognizing Your hand at work in my life."

ABOVE-THE-LINE THINKING

Set your mind on things above, not on things on the earth.

— Colossians 3:2

Traditionally speaking, some of us think that "setting our minds on things above" refers to the second coming of the Lord—that is, what is going on in Heaven. We assume it has something to do with eschatology and end-time events, and that may be true, but "setting our minds on things above" has a more practical, everyday meaning as well.

When we set our minds on things above, we start thinking about the things that happen to us the way Heaven thinks about them. When something painful happens in our lives, what is happening in Heaven? What is God doing? What is He thinking? What is He showing us? What is happening in the spiritual realm as this particular event occurs?

Some of us have been hurt by our children. What does Heaven think about that? Some of us have been hurt by the church—what is happening in Heaven surrounding the events that caused us pain?

Setting our minds on things above means that we are responding the way Heaven is responding. It is easy to respond out of our own pain, emotions, thought processes, and intense feelings of being insulted or betrayed: "How dare they do that to me? Who do they think they are?" But that is not heavenly thinking. What *is* heavenly thinking? It is asking ourselves, *What is God trying to accomplish by allowing certain things to happen to me?*

As we start thinking that way, something remarkable happens—the things holding us back disappear.

The result of your choices will be spiritual or earthly.

CONTEMPLATIONS

Spiritual choices grow into spiritual habits,
while earthly choices grow into earthly habits.
Do painful events seem to happen repeatedly to you?
Ask God to reveal any earthly habits
He wants to change within you.

The fruit of the Spirit displayed through your actions
and character attract Heaven's help.
On a daily basis, are you pleased with your responses?
What do you think needs to happen in order for you
to become more pleased with them?

For everyone born of God overcomes the world.
This is the victory that has overcome the world, even our faith.
— 1 JOHN 5:4 NIV

Chapter 4

THE MOMENT OF CHOICE

Which Will Rule You—the Spirit or the Soul?

We live in a battle zone, and most of us aren't even conscious of its existence.

A constant battle wages between the spirit and the soul, and everything that happens to us is a *stimulus* trying to push us one way or the other. It is a stimulus when we spill coffee all over our laps. It is a stimulus when someone runs a red light and almost totals our car. It is a stimulus when someone gives us a compliment. We recognize stimuli because our hearts beat a little faster.

We typically respond to stimuli in one of two ways: in a way that builds up the soul (the mind, will, and emotions) or in a way that builds up the spirit (wisdom, communion, and conscience). With every stimulus, there will be some sort of response, even if that response is a decision *not* to respond. Here is what we need to remember: our response comes not from the stimulus itself but from the choice we made the moment after the stimulus occurred.

23

In between the stimulus and the response is a nanosecond of time that psychologists call the "moment of choice." This is the space of time in which choices are made. The more we recognize this moment of choice, the broader and longer it seems to be. In a way, time itself seems to drop into slow motion. If you've ever been in a car accident, you know how everything appears to slow down around that moment of impact, and you can remember incredible detail. That is similar to what happens at the moment of choice as we begin to recognize it—the moment slows down. Conversely, the more prone we are to react in heat and anger, fear, or some other type of emotion, the shorter the moment of choice becomes.

The moment of choice determines whether we say "yes" to the spirit or "yes" to the soul. That choice we make in the moment will determine if God is justified in acting on our behalf or if He isn't. If we respond soulishly, giving in to the anger, we further remove ourselves from the good God has for us. Sin distances us from Him; it essentially erects a temporary wall between us and what God would like to do for us.

But on the other end of the spectrum, any spiritual choice we make brings us closer to God and allows Him to justifiably act on our behalf—and act often.

WHAT DO YOU WANT?

The first moment of choice in Scripture occurs in Genesis 3:12–14:

> Then the man said, "The woman whom You gave to be with me, she gave me of the tree, and I ate."
>
> And the Lord God said to the woman, "What is this you have done?" The woman said, "The serpent deceived me, and I ate."

So the LORD God said to the serpent: "Because you have done this . . ."

Adam and Eve were presented with choices in the moment of their temptation, and God held each of them individually responsible for the choices they made.

We face multiple moments of choice every day. Some of them we are able to recognize, and some of them we aren't—at least not today, but we will be able to in the future. Some of them result in soul-based decisions because we feel justified in our response. The man cut off in traffic by a bad driver has a moment of choice, and it can be difficult for him to make a good, spirit-based choice because he feels justified in reacting in anger. Our eyes can be locked on God and His Holy Spirit, looking to do what will please Him, or we can be focused on ourselves by expressing un-Christlike behavior. We can be Kingdom minded or empire minded.

Paul described the moment of choice in Romans 7:14–18:

> For we know that the law is spiritual, but I am carnal, sold under sin. For what I am doing, I do not understand. For what I will to do, that I do not practice; but what I hate, that I do. If, then, I do what I will not to do, I agree with the law that it is good. But now, it is no longer I who do it, but sin that dwells in me. For I know that in me (that is, in my flesh) nothing good dwells; for to will is present with me, but how to perform what is good I do not find.

Paul called it the flesh—not physical flesh, as in the human body, but the carnal flesh; the Greek word is *psuche*. The soul wars against the spirit because, obviously, the soul wants to make a soulish choice.

25

The spirit, meanwhile, wants to make a spiritual choice, following after the Spirit of God, and the two war against each other. Paul wrote, "For what I will to do, that I do not practice; but what I hate, that I do." This is war. The spirit and the soul are at war during the moment of choice.

The soul says, "You're justified. Just do it."

The spirit says, "Don't do it. There are unintended consequences if you do that."

Perceiving which is which is difficult in the beginning, but as we become more spiritually led, the moment of choice widens until it seems like it is a mile long. When the spirit leads us, it is like finding one of those proverbial "holes" on the football field—it just opens up in front of the quarterback, and he walks right into the end zone. No one even touched him because the opening was so wide.

Yet when we are led by the soul, the moment of choice gets smaller and smaller until it is almost undetectable. The enemy wants us to fail to recognize it so we make a choice that does not align with the Spirit of God.

"Hit him back."

"Exaggerate some error she made. She deserves it."

"Come up with a scheme to show him that he's not so big."

"Catch him doing something and retaliate."

Soulish choices tend to make us like little gods, because we judge and carry out the sentence. The more choices we make from the soul, the less noticeable the moment of choice becomes. What should be a choice becomes more of a reaction, like a doctor checking our reflexes.

WE SEE THROUGH A FILTER

The moment of choice has incredible power over our futures. We won't be able to build a history of private victories without succeeding in the moment of choice. Private victories are the "small" things we do because God told us to do them.

"I don't want you to swear at the person who just cut you off in traffic."

"All right, God. I won't do it."

"I want you to be kind to your waitress today at lunch."

"All right, God. I will do it."

The examples could go on and on, but in every one of them, this small choice always seems untimely and insignificant. These choices from God are not about the specific action you take (i.e., "Be kind to the waitress") but about obedience. Obedience is a great attractor to Heaven's help.

Private victories are like small grains of sand that, when surrounded by the concrete of the Holy Spirit, form a foundation that can withstand the weight of public victory. We can't have public victories without succeeding in the moment of choice, nor can we live righteously without succeeding in the moment of choice. Making spiritual choices in the moment of choice produces a righteous life. The moment of choice determines where we go in life, the level of gifting we walk in, how we hear from God, and how we relate to God and one another. We are either going to walk in the Spirit—in wisdom, communion, and conscience—or we are going to walk in the soul, relying on the human mind, will, and emotions.

In every situation, we see the stimulus through a filter, and that filter is either the filter of the spirit or the filter of the soul. Filters are like sunglasses we wear that tell us how we should perceive a situation. The Spirit says, "But for My grace, this would have happened to you last week. What they did to you, you would have done to somebody else last week, but I stopped it. You almost ran a red light, but I caught your attention just in time, and you stopped." That is an example of a spiritual filter that leads to a spiritual reaction.

The soulish reaction is anger—chasing the car, trying to catch up with the driver, any number of things to let people know they did something wrong. And that is the wrong choice. If we make soulish decisions, we shorten the "gap" of the moment of choice and darken our eyes to what the Holy Spirit is doing.

The goal is to live a spiritual life, so our filters will be spiritual and we will see through spiritual eyes. As that goal is met, each step we take draws us deeper into the Spirit of God and increases our chances to make spiritual decisions, spiritual choices, and produce the spiritual fruit Paul was talking about in Galatians 5:22–23:

> But the fruit of the Spirit is love, joy, peace, longsuffering, kindness, goodness, faithfulness, gentleness, self-control. Against such there is no law.

If I might paraphrase, Paul was saying, "Don't just talk the things of the Spirit—walk a life in the Spirit. Make it real in your life. This is not just a good idea; it can be a way of living that benefits you and everyone around you."

As we walk in the Spirit and make the moment-by-moment choices to live spiritual lives, our ability to perceive what the Holy Spirit is doing will increase. We won't miss as many of the intricacies of His hand—the small movements, the details. We will know Him at a deep, intimate level, where the cry of our hearts becomes, "Let me live in Your shadow. Let me breathe, move, and have my being in You, because only then will I be fully alive."

In summary, we have the ability to choose. We have an independent will, and the soul and spirit are both after our will, trying to rule it. Therefore, we exercise self-discipline in order to cause the will to be subordinate to the spirit, which is hard to do. Early in our efforts to make spiritual choices, we often fail to distinguish the difference between the soul and spirit, and so we think that the soul is the spirit and the spirit is the soul. But that will quickly change.

It is time to change our thinking. And as we change our thinking, at the end of the day, we will be able to look at God and smile and say, "I see You."

CONTEMPLATIONS

The choice we make at the moment of stimulus
will determine how much God is justified in acting on our behalf.
What "filters" keep you from making
consistent spiritual responses?

Private victories are the small grains of sand that,
when covered by the Holy Spirit, give us a strong foundation
that can withstand the weight of public victory.
What was your last private victory?
What was it?

Your will be done
On earth as it is in heaven.
—MATTHEW 6:10

Chapter 5

THE KINGDOM IS WITHIN YOU

How God Changes You from the Inside Out

The Kingdom of God is not solely a New Testament concept. The coming rule and reign of God's Kingdom is interwoven throughout the fabric of the Old Testament like fine gold threads in a king's tapestry. We see an eternal, living God who rules over the affairs of humankind:

> For the kingdom is the LORD's,
> And He rules over the nations.
> — PSALM 22:28

> He rules by His power forever;
> His eyes observe the nations;
> Do not let the rebellious exalt themselves.
> — PSALM 66:7

The LORD has established His throne in heaven,
And His kingdom rules over all.
— PSALM 103:19

For unto us a Child is born,
Unto us a Son is given;
And the government will be upon His shoulder.
And His name will be called
Wonderful, Counselor, Mighty God,
Everlasting Father, Prince of Peace.
Of the increase of His government and peace
There will be no end,
Upon the throne of David and over His kingdom,
To order it and establish it with judgment and justice
From that time forward, even forever.
The zeal of the LORD of hosts will perform this.
— ISAIAH 9:6–7

We know several things about this God who introduces Himself to humanity in the Old Testament. One, He is daily involved in human affairs and periodically reveals Himself in strange and mighty ways to human beings.

Moses understood the need for God's presence and help to reach the promised land:

Now therefore, I pray, if I have found grace in Your sight, show me now Your way, that I may know You and that I may find grace in Your sight. And consider that this nation is Your people.

— EXODUS 33:13

Daniel understood that there comes a time when human choices have been made and weighed by Heaven's agents, and in every case, the ultimate authority is God Himself:

> This decision is by the decree of the watchers,
> And the sentence by the word of the holy ones,
> In order that the living may know
> That the Most High rules in the kingdom of men,
> Gives it to whomever He will,
> And sets over it the lowest of men.
> —DANIEL 4:17

In addition, it is clear that this God who reveals Himself has a purpose for the human race:

> So God created man in His own image; in the image of God
> He created him; male and female He created them. Then God
> blessed them, and God said to them, "Be fruitful and multiply;
> fill the earth and subdue it; have dominion over the fish of the
> sea, over the birds of the air, and over every living thing that
> moves on the earth."
> —GENESIS 1:27–28

When humanity as a whole failed to achieve their ordained purpose, God temporarily narrowed His focus to one nation: Israel. And when that nation also failed, He looked to one Man: Jesus Christ. Prophets began to speak of the day when people would live together in peace (Isaiah 2:4); problems would be solved; death, sorrow, and sickness would be abolished; and even the animal kingdom would be at peace with one another (Isaiah 11:6). They perceived the Kingdom from afar.

God's Kingdom came to earth as a single event—the appearance of Jesus the Messiah, who had much to say about the Kingdom. He "bent" the minds of those who had studied Scripture all their lives and thought they knew everything that could be known about God:

> Now when He was asked by the Pharisees when the kingdom of God would come, He answered them and said, "The kingdom of God does not come with observation; nor will they say, 'See here!' or 'See there!' For indeed, the kingdom of God is within you."
>
> — LUKE 17:20-21

In the minds of the Pharisees, the Kingdom of God meant the rule of God upon the earth. Essentially, they were asking Jesus, "When are You going to take over Rome? Throw down our oppressor for us!"

But Jesus answered, "The Kingdom of God does not come with observation." In other words, the Kingdom of God is not a spectator sport. They weren't going to see an army rise up to overthrow Rome on their behalf. Instead, when they were able to change their thinking and develop a right, true relationship with God, they would see that the Kingdom was within them. The God of the Old Testament was doing something new on the earth. Everything was about to change.

THE KINGDOM AND YOUR THOUGHT LIFE

> A good man out of the good treasure of his heart brings forth good; and an evil man out of the evil treasure of his heart brings forth evil. For out of the abundance of the heart his mouth speaks.
>
> — LUKE 6:45

The more "Kingdom" we are in our thinking, the lighter, more golden, more full of God, more holy, and more pure our thinking becomes. Typically what happens is that we have incredible times of *high* Kingdom thinking, when we make excellent choices, but then the pendulum swings, and we come close to dark thinking. We swing back to high thinking and then veer back down toward dark thinking. Our Father understands us more than we understand ourselves, and He will be faithful to perfect that which He began in us (Philippians 1:6). While we may vacillate between greater and lesser thinking, as long as He is our focus, we are on a steady march toward becoming more like Him, with purer Kingdom thinking. That is the eventual outcome of our vacillation as we walk through day-to-day life, sometimes with great faith and sometimes not.

If the Kingdom of God is "within" us, as Jesus said in Luke 17, then we make *interior* choices before *exterior* results are seen. In other words, we have to change on the inside before we get the behavior we want on the outside. First our hearts change; then our thoughts begin to change, and out of changed thoughts come changed actions. And when others see we have changed, they, too, will change.

It is interesting to me how even Jesus' death, burial, resurrection, and ascension reflect the way He brings change. After His death on the cross, He had business to take care of. Scripture tells us what happened—He went *internal*. Ephesians 4 says He "descended into the earth," and Peter wrote that He proclaimed the good news in Hades (1 Peter 3:19). Do you see what is happening here? We are made of the dust of this earth, and deep into the earth was the first place Jesus went. God first goes deep before He tries to change the exterior, for the Kingdom of God *is within you.*

As we realize the ways of God and how He begins His great work within us, we start to understand why we sometimes experience emotional turmoil in our lives. God wants to get rid of the things within us that are unholy, and I guarantee you that every time we are about to go to the next level, we will experience the *regeneration* of soulish things we thought we had conquered. Why? Because He is going *deeper* in order to remove what would harm us at the next spiritual level. He always deals with our weakness before He promotes us so that when the promotion comes, the weakness doesn't destroy us. We can get away with certain things in the Outer Courtyard that would decimate us in the Holy of Holies.

Therefore, when we are facing difficulty we need to ask ourselves if we are in the situation because God is moving. That realization isn't always easy to make. We tend to say, "Please pray for me, because the enemy is really attacking me." We don't see what else it could be—that God might be allowing the difficulty in order to reveal what needs to be conquered in us before we are promoted.

God's Kingdom is like Him; it is strong and purposeful. Everything He does, He does for a reason. He is not up in Heaven shaking His head and telling nearby angels, "Oh, My goodness—I'd better hurry. John Paul's in trouble." No, He sometimes allows the enemy to reveal what I need to work on, and then as He and I work on it, He tells me, "Well done, good and faithful servant. You have been faithful in the little things; now I am going to promote you."

We would like for the process to be different. We would like for promotion to come quickly and for all potential problems to be kept away from us. But in the Kingdom, it is God's mercy to promote us after He has healed the things that could harm us—it is His mercy that allows difficulty in our lives. We could say it this way: He wants to put good wine in a good wineskin, so it doesn't tear us apart. He does this so "both are preserved" (Matthew 9:17).

Here are three important questions to ask yourself when you're experiencing difficult times:

- What is happening in the invisible realm as I deal with this problem?

- Why am I dealing with this problem?

- What is God trying to do?

The Kingdom perceives things that are not as though they were (Romans 4:17). We need to start thinking along the same lines and see the way our lives will be after this momentary affliction is over. *What will it be like once I've conquered this thing that God is dealing with in my life?* The affliction is real, but the purpose and result are not yet seen. No matter what occurs in our lives, we can know a good result is coming because the justice of God will see that it comes.

What do we do in the meantime? We stand at the door and knock. We ask Him for what we need, and we keep asking Him, and we believe.

First the Kingdom is internal. Then it is external.

In John 20:22, Jesus breathed on His disciples and said, "Receive the Holy Spirit." He brought something from the *inside* of Him to the *outside* of Him. As He breathed and they inhaled, the Spirit went *internal.* He then sent these men out to change the world. Demons were cast out, sickness was healed, lepers were cleansed, the dead were raised—amazing things happened when Jesus blew the breath of God into His disciples. The world changed. The disciples performed miracles and told people, "The Kingdom of God has come near you."

THE EXTERNAL MANIFESTATION OF THE KINGDOM

As with the internal nature of the Kingdom, the external manifestation of the Kingdom is vitally important. It displays the reality of God's Kingdom and its rule over every other kingdom:

> As they went out, behold, they brought to Him a man, mute and demon-possessed. And when the demon was cast out, the mute spoke. And the multitudes marveled, saying, "It was never seen like this in Israel!" But the Pharisees said, "He casts out demons by the ruler of the demons." Then Jesus went about all the cities and villages, teaching in their synagogues, preaching the gospel of the kingdom, and healing every sickness and every disease among the people.
>
> — MATTHEW 9:32–35

The Pharisees accused Jesus of casting out demons by the ruler of demons, and Jesus essentially replied, "Do you think that's something? Watch this!" The manifestation of the Kingdom was within Him, and with the outer manifestation He let others know that it could be within them as well.

The Kingdom is within you. Right now. In this moment. Are you aware of it?

CONTEMPLATIONS

The Kingdom is within us.
This means our internal choices don't always
produce quick external results.
We often have to wait to see the changes we want in our lives.
Right now, what change are you hoping to see in your life?
Are you trusting God to finish the work He started in you?

God always deals with our weaknesses before promoting us;
otherwise, the next level could defeat us.
What is God working on in you?
What Scripture has He given you to help you
through the season you're in?

Chapter 6

SEEING THE UNSEEN

Maximizing Heaven's Help

Right now, as you sit here with this book in your hands, you are surrounded by the realm of the unseen.

That realm includes Heaven's hosts, the different rankings of angels throughout the angelic authority structure, as well as other spiritual beings of God—ones we don't know much about because they are mentioned only a few times in Scripture. They are here even when we aren't aware of it, and it is possible to position ourselves to maximize their help in our lives. We can be in a place where God's creation, human and non-human, can act on our behalf—where the co-existing spiritual world takes action to see the plans of God come about.

In 2 Kings 6, the king of Syria was making war against Israel, and Elisha the prophet knew his plans; the Lord revealed to Elisha what the enemy was about to do. The king's attendants somehow found out about

Elisha and told their master, "It is as if he sees into our room and knows what we are doing."

That, of course, didn't make the king particularly happy, and he sent an army to kill Elisha. But look at what happened:

> Therefore he sent horses and chariots and a great army there, and they came by night and surrounded the city. And when the servant of the man of God [Elisha] arose early and went out, there was an army, surrounding the city with horses and chariots. And his servant said to him, "Alas, my master! What shall we do?" So he answered, "Do not fear, for those who are with us are more than those who are with them." And Elisha prayed, and said, "Lord, I pray, open his eyes that he may see." Then the Lord opened the eyes of the young man, and he saw. And behold, the mountain was full of horses and chariots of fire all around Elisha. So when the Syrians came down to him, Elisha prayed to the Lord, and said, "Strike this people, I pray, with blindness." And He struck them with blindness according to the word of Elisha.
>
> — 2 Kings 6:14–18

Wouldn't you agree that, in that moment, Elisha maximized Heaven's help?

That was a major attack, a physical onslaught by a "great" army. Who knows how many soldiers stood against him? It was likely several thousand, but Elisha didn't bat an eye. Instead, he spoke one of the most powerful statements in Scripture:

"Do not fear, for those who are with us are more than those who are with them."

Sometimes I feel like a "great" army has been sent after me. It could have physical properties such as a friend who hurts me, a minister who ridicules me, or an unexpected diagnosis. It could come in any number of ways and forms. But whether I see it or not, there is spiritual activity going on around me to help me get through the difficult times. Elisha knew that, and he positioned himself to be in the right place before God, trusting His care, which allowed Heaven to take action on Elisha's behalf.

In every issue of our lives, every day, there are hosts, numerous angels, fire, and armies of Heaven around us. The servant didn't see it—but Elisha did. Whether we see it or not has no bearing on whether it is there. However, if we want to *maximize* the help God would give us, we have to come to the place where we, like Elisha, believe that the spiritual realm is more impacting and vastly superior to the physical realm.

If the physical realm has the potential to impact us, then the spiritual realm has the potential for even greater impact. If this were not true, the spiritual realm wouldn't have been able to afflict the Syrian army with blindness, but based on this story, we can see that the spiritual realm is the greater realm. Remember that not one angel has ever been hurt—or even bruised—by a human.

The problem most of us run into is one of sight. We don't "see" the spiritual realm, so we don't "know" that it is waiting to help us. We might have a general understanding that more exists than what we see, but we usually don't remember that when times are tough, and if we can't remember it, it is very difficult to appropriate it.

BE CAREFUL WHERE YOU PUT YOUR EYES

When Elisha's servant saw the human armies that had come to kill his master, he reacted with fear. "We are in *big* trouble! This is our day to die." His spiritual paralysis kept him from *seeing*.

Fear does us no favors. At best, it spiritually paralyzes us. It takes our eyes off of God and causes us to focus on our circumstances. If we allow fear to control our thoughts, we actually empower the enemy by creating room for him to operate in our lives. There are times when fear can sound like wisdom, and we can find ourselves steeped in fear when we are trying to "think rationally."

"My company is downsizing. What if they let me go?"

"What if this job opportunity falls flat?"

"What if God really wanted me to buy the other house, and buying this house was a mistake?"

What if, what if . . . ? If we *think* on the oh-no's, we will get the oh-no's.

God has given us the blueprints for the type of thinking that will produce a Kingdom mind-set. Paul clearly revealed this in Philippians 4:8:

> Whatever things are true, whatever things are noble, what-ever things are just, whatever things are pure, whatever things are lovely, whatever things are of good report, if there is any virtue and if there is anything praiseworthy—meditate on these things.

When our eyes are on Jesus, we get Jesus. As we think on things that are praiseworthy and just, we will be able to say, "Even if something 'bad' happens, it will be all right. I know something better is in store for me, because I know my God." We trust in God with all our hearts. We lean not on our own understanding. Our focus changes *because we know our God!*

As we seek first His Kingdom and His righteousness, we begin to know Him. He moves from being merely a divine "shadow" in His Word to being a real entity with a personality, thoughts, feelings—Someone we can touch. Someone we can know. Someone we can develop a relationship with and a history.

The servant reacted with fear, but when Elisha saw the army that had come to kill him, he proclaimed, "Oh, you are so not going to win." He knew that there was nothing unaddressed in his life that would prohibit God from acting on his behalf—so God would take action and deliver Elisha from his affliction.

Elisha knew the protection God had arranged for him. He perceived the heavenly army; therefore, when the prophet prayed, God used the power of those invisible armies to afflict the Syrians. That is called the Kingdom of God. It is growing in our lives, and we can expand it even more by learning to think in Kingdom ways.

The prophet had a very simple solution for his servant who could not see; he reached over and prayed for him, asking God to open the man's eyes. What I am hoping and praying will happen as you read this book is that God will begin to open your eyes so you have faith to see the unseen—faith to believe the unbelievable, faith to acknowledge the armies of Heaven all around you, waiting to take action. It is difficult for those armies to take action on our behalf if we don't really believe they are there.

Remember, God will move on our behalf if we ask . . . because we believe Him. If we don't believe, it will be difficult to ask Him for help. We need to begin to change our thinking. In order for us to change our thinking, we need to know what we are supposed to think about, which we will discuss in greater detail in the next chapter.

CONTEMPLATIONS

God has already sent His army to save you.
Have you ever asked God to reveal the army
He's sent to protect and fight for you?

The spiritual realm is far superior to the physical realm.
Would truly believing that statement change
the way you think about your circumstances?

Chapter 7

BEHOLD, PEOPLE OF LIGHT

It's More Than a Metaphor

If God is all-knowing, which He is, then Christians should be the most enlightened people on the face of the earth. Jesus actually calls us the light of the world, and Paul wrote that in this world we "shine like stars" (Philippians 2:15 NCV). Over and over again, God describes Himself as light, and we take after Him the way children take after their father. If anyone is enlightened on this planet, it should be us because logically speaking, only those who follow the true Light can become "enlightened."

ENLIGHTENED THINKING

The words that I speak to you are spirit, and they are life.

— John 6:63

In the Garden of Eden, there were two trees. One brought death and the other brought life. The Tree of Knowledge of Good and Evil is the tree of this world. The world's spiritual leaders may have climbed this tree higher than anyone else, but it is still the wrong tree. Every decision we make from that tree—from the soul—strengthens the soul and darkens the paths of our thinking.

The Tree of Life, however, could also be called the Tree of the Spirit. When we make decisions based on that tree, we make spiritual choices that open us to the Spirit and draw us closer to our Father.

Relatively speaking, very few people climb high on the Tree of Life. And those of us who make the attempt usually think the bottom branches are the top, because we don't look up to see where we are going. Instead, we look down to see where we have been. "Look how high I am! I am so much more spiritual than I used to be!" Or we look down at the people below us and say, "I can't believe I used to react that way."

As long as we keep looking down to see where we were, we will never see the possibilities that await us—how high we can still go. There are all sorts of nooks and crannies and cliffs and high places and adventures to explore in this Kingdom of God. Much of our current church culture teaches us to look down to see where we have come from—but God wants us to look up to see where we are going.

The Tree of Life is the tree of *light*. When we eat from it, we become enlightened. If we eat from the wrong tree, we become "endarkened," all the while thinking we are becoming enlightened. That is the greatest deception—thinking dark is light and light is dark. Satan tempted Adam and Eve by telling them, "Eat of this tree and you will gain knowledge. You will become like God. You will know what God knows, so you can become like Him." That is basically what every religion except Judaic

Christianity teaches: a person can become like God or even become God Himself.

Yes, God wants us to be like Him, but we do so through the blood of His Son and the work of the Holy Spirit within us. It is a gift, one accepted by faith. Knowledge does not constitute the light. If it did, revival would have begun in secular universities millennia ago. Intellect does not constitute the light. If it did, only the most intelligent would be able to know God, and those of us who are "average" would not be able to know Him. But that is not how it works. You can't be enlightened unless you have access to the light, and if you don't serve the light, you can't have access to the light.

The apostle John put it like this: "Whoever has been born of God does not sin, for his seed remains in him; and he cannot sin, because he has been born of God" (1 John 3:9). The Greek word for "seed" is *sperma*, which is the root of our word *sperm*. It is the same sperm that unites with the egg to produce an embryo, and nine months later, a baby is born. This seed of God produces change; we literally are born of Him, and when He calls us the light of the world (Matthew 5:14), it is not a metaphor. God is light, so those of us who are born from His seed are children of Light. Again, the only people who can be truly enlightened are those who have been born from the one true Light—God.

Jesus told the Pharisees, "You are of your father the devil." They had chosen the world's darkness over the light of God, and in making that choice, they were reborn, conceived in the *sperma* of darkness. Each of us walks that same road until we are called "out of darkness into His marvelous light" (1 Peter 2:9). When we are saved, we are rebirthed through the *sperma* of light. We become born again as God transitions us from the realm of darkness into the Kingdom of His light, and we become His actual sons and daughters.

FOCUS ON THE LIGHT

Physically speaking, what does light do? When light enters a room, shadows dissipate and the room gets brighter. If we are the light of the world, everywhere we go becomes brighter, more illumined, and warmer. The world encounters the light, and as a moth is attracted to light, others will be attracted to you . . . if you do not hide your light.

The children of God are called to enlighten the world (Matthew 5:14). We have a greater authority and power than the world does, but as we talked about in the last chapter, if we don't believe what God has said, how will we be able to walk in the authority and power available to us? If we don't *believe* that He who is in us is greater than the enemy, how will we be able to believe that our light can make a difference in the world?

A number of years ago, the Lord impressed upon me, "What you focus on you will make room for." To "make room" means we have to push something else aside. We make room for what has our attention, and where we put our "ears" is just as important as where we put our "eyes." If I allow myself to listen to the enemy, I begin making room for the enemy by pushing God aside, and the result is worry. All the negative things that *could* happen begin to swamp me, and soon I am consumed with fear and anxiety, because I have become focused on a string of hypothetical scenarios that *could* happen. The power of God seems to shrink in those moments because I've taken my focus off of Him. I am not listening to Him. Once fear has my attention, it starts to grow and build momentum. But when I turn and put my attention on God, the fear starts to shrink. I replace the lies of the enemy with the truth of God.

That is one reason I don't like speaking to demonic forces when I pray—I know I need to be careful where I put my attention. Whenever I do have to deal with darkness, I don't allow myself to focus on the darkness; instead, I focus on the power of God to remove the enemy. That is yet another everyday application of Matthew 6:33: "Seek first the kingdom of God and His righteousness, and all these things shall be added to you." The light needs to be our focus, not the darkness.

Similarly, I try not to look for what the enemy is doing in another person's life. What good would that do? I do not wish to focus on the darkness, so I try to look for the light. I look at the people around me with this filter: "What is God's purpose for your life? What is God doing in you? What does God see when He looks at you?" I'm much more interested in how God sees you. I want to see what He sees. I do not want to judge after the flesh but after the Spirit.

The Light reveals all things. It is a compass in the storm. It is hope. It is our foundation. I want to see what is real, according to the light of God.

CONTEMPLATIONS

What you focus on you make room for.
Are you investing enough of your thought life
into the plans and purposes of God?
Are you clearing out the necessary space for a big God to do big things?

Focus on the light.
Look at the people around you through this lens:
"What is God's purpose for your life?
What is God doing with you?"

Chapter 8

Luck Has Nothing to Do with It

Recognizing the Hidden Hand of God

Anyone who has heard me speak or taken my courses knows how much I love Acts 17:26–28. The first part of the passage says:

> And He has made from one blood every nation of men to dwell on the face of the earth, and has determined their pre-appointed times and the boundaries of their dwellings.

Why would God go to the trouble of choosing the exact places we would live? This passage reveals that the Creator of all things—the One who holds all things together, for whom all things were created and in whom all things consist—looks through time to see each of His children. He sees the details of the world in a way our minds cannot possibly grasp, and He says, "I know what I am doing with My son Bill. I am going to put Bill in Scottsdale, Arizona, on this specific day, in this specific year, because there is something for him to do, and only he can do it as well as it needs to be done. Bill walks in My light, and he is a carrier of My light."

God has a plan for your life, and that plan is detailed, and it is special, and it involves His light. Your light in the midst of darkness will bring change to the people who dwell in darkness. Concerning the Messiah, Isaiah wrote that those who lived in darkness would see a marvelous, incredible, life-changing light. You carry that same light within you! When your light dwells in the midst of darkness, you become a point of change for people, because the Giver of all life flows out from you to touch them.

The second part of my beloved passage in Acts reveals more of God's thought process—why He does what He does with our lives:

So that they should seek the Lord, in the hope that they might grope for Him and find Him, though He is not far from each one of us; for in Him we live and move and have our being, as also some of your own poets have said, "For we are also His offspring."

Finding God is a powerful thing. It changes you. It brings you out of darkness, and even if you feel that you are groping to find Him, His light within you influences other people toward Him.

Everywhere you go, remember that you have an impact on people. At one level or another, people will recognize when you are with them. The very Spirit of the living God is within you, and the earth itself recognizes when its Creator is present. You have an impact even on the land under your feet because of the presence of the Creator within you. Darkness will recognize when you are present because you are full of light, and it is nothing but a fading shadow. This is a vital aspect of walking in the knowledge and ways of God.

THE LAW OF OBSERVATION

The law of observation is the ability to look at something and change it. It is an actual law found in nature. Scientific studies in quantum mechanics such as the Young Experiment have discovered that electrons, the subatomic particles found in atoms, move in the direction anticipated by the observer. In other words, they spin the way you expect them to spin. You can change the spin of an electron by the expectation you have when observing it. In scientific communities this phenomenon is called the observer effect.

As we consider the law of observation on a broad scale, we realize something shocking. If all creation is made up of atoms and all atoms have electrons orbiting within them, then we have the ability to look at the lives of the people around us and change them, just by how we perceive them. My sons will start to become what I believe them to be; they will gradually come to complement my vision of them. If other people are around me long enough, they will form a habit of being whatever I think they are, and that habit can begin to affect how they interact with other people.

IT ISN'T LUCK

Your vision or view of others must be matched by how you treat them, as well as the time you spend with them. If I am not unified in my perspective and actions, it will create a schism in me and eventually in the people I am observing. That is the power of leadership, of fatherhood—people become how you view them. They carry what you perceive them to be outside the walls of your church, your business, your home, far outside your influence on them. They form a habit of being a certain way, good or bad. Negative or positive. Life giving or not life giving.

If I can affect the people around me by perceiving them a certain way—then I want to be careful how I think! I want to view people the way God created them. I want to look where those people are going, not just where they are now, so when they are around me, they long to be what God created them to be. I want them to start asking, *What has God created me for?* If asking that question becomes a habit when they are with me, they will keep asking it even when they leave my presence. They will begin to think, *I can get there! I can make it!* Observing those around you in light of God's purpose creates an atmosphere of hope. It's one of the more overlooked traits among effective leaders.

Too many of us have been raised with a subtle, hidden understanding that we can't make it, or that if we do make it, we are just really lucky. We think this way because our focus has been set on the wrong things. If we focus on pain, loss, and the way life has beaten us down, we make room for more pain and greater discouragement. But we don't have to live that way. That is not how God views our lives. It is possible for us to change the progression; we can stop and go in a different direction. We can change the way we view ourselves and others, and we can make room for destiny and God's purposes to happen.

THE WAY YOU SEE YOU

Cast down every vain imagination, and cast
down every argument that exalts itself
against the knowledge of God.

— 2 Corinthians 10:5, paraphrase

The "knowledge of God" is very specific in the Greek language; it means God's knowledge and understanding about His creation, of which we are a part. As God's creation, we need to think about ourselves the way He thinks about us. You need to think about you the way God thinks about you. Just as the law of observation affects the people around me, it also affects how you view yourself (Proverbs 23:7).

See yourself the way God sees you. Why did He put you here? What is His intended purpose? Are you living the way God created you to live and the way God sees you? God sees you in light of where you are going. Yes, He recognizes where you are today, but He also sees you in light of the future He has for you. It is the Jeremiah 29:11 principle: "I know the plans that I have for you . . . plans for a future, plans to give you hope" NIV.

Your life is not a matter of luck, good or bad. It is never luck. God has a plan, and as you begin to see the telltale motions of His hand in your life, you will be amazed.

God has a good future for you—how can you align yourself with God and pursue His future in a positive way? It starts by changing the way you see you.

CONTEMPLATIONS

You become what you think about yourself.
What is the most encouraging and empowering thought
you've ever had about yourself?
Make that thought a habit!

You have an impact on people everywhere you go.
You can cause them to feel hope just by being in their presence.
Have you ever noticed a change in the atmosphere
when you or someone else walked into the room?

Chapter 9

A CLOSER LOOK AT THE KINGDOM

Revealing God's Kingdom to the World

If the goal is to be Kingdom minded, what is the Kingdom? Historically, some have thought the Kingdom was simply a personal prayer relationship between God and man that can be summated in the Lord's Prayer: "Thy Kingdom come, thy will be done." Some have thought it was the Church itself—that the Kingdom is the Church. Others have thought it was an aspect of eternity and life after death, a time when we live in the continued sight of Jesus. Albert Schweitzer thought it was a future reality when time stopped and a new heavenly order began. St. Augustine thought it was the rule of the Church that would eventually cover the entire earth. Each of these traditional ideas is *partly* true.

Currently, much of the Church assumes the Kingdom of God to have two basic aspects: the Church itself and the individual. But the Church as an organization cannot actually be "the Kingdom," for if it were, no one could be healed outside the four walls of a church, and we know that it isn't the case. People experience the healing nature of Jesus outside the church all the time. Jesus said that the Kingdom is inside each of us, so in my words, the Church is an outgrowth, or the result, of the manifestation of the Kingdom within us. It is the *instrument* and community of the Kingdom.

THE INVISIBLE KINGDOM

The Kingdom cannot be seen with the natural eye, though the results of the Kingdom can be seen.

Gravity is an example of a natural law where an invisible force affects the visible world. We can't *see* gravity, yet it clearly is part of our reality. When you drop a pen, an unseen force pulls it to the floor. If you jump over a chair, you will come down on the other side. Just as the invisible force of gravity impacts and governs everything on earth, so does the Kingdom. Every time we pray, we are indirectly invoking the spiritual laws of Heaven to release its forces—the Lord's hosts and the rest of Heaven's agents—to act on our behalf.

The Lord's Prayer reveals the heart behind all prayer: "Your Kingdom come and Your will be done." Every prayer we pray to God centers on that point. The prayer is more than just a repetition of the words, "Your Kingdom come"—it is what *encompasses* "Your Kingdom come." The Lord's Prayer invokes, substantiates, and fully recognizes the spiritual law of the Kingdom. When we pray the Lord's Prayer, we have done something of great worth, something mysterious, something we don't always realize we have done. The world around us begins to bend as the power of God's Kingdom on earth increases.

Over the years, I have learned that the Kingdom message must be accompanied by miracles, signs, and wonders. Jesus' mighty works were intended to prove that the Kingdom of God had come near. Mark 9:35 says that He preached the gospel of the Kingdom and healed every sickness and disease—every one of them. Without signs of God's power, people scatter and don't rally to the Kingdom cause, because there is no evidence of the Kingdom. We haven't shown them anything that proves the Kingdom. It is no wonder that those in the New Age movement don't believe in the Kingdom to come or in life after death, outside of reincarnation. They don't believe because we haven't shown them anything that proves otherwise. We must have God's power to prove that the rest of what we say is true. Without power, I can't blame the world for not believing us.

When presented with a Jesus without signs and miracles, the world mentally dissects the situation: *Well, the wisdom of the Christians is a type of wisdom, but I have another type of wisdom, and my friend has another, and all of our wisdom put together makes a collective "God-consciousness."* Until we have power that goes with our words, they have a right to believe those things, because we cannot show them anything different. We need the power of God to be manifested on earth in order for them to believe that God exists and they need Him.

When people can see God's power, the Kingdom advances. Paul understood this from his encounter with Jesus, and he wrote in 1 Corinthians 2:4–5:

> My speech and my preaching were not with persuasive words
> of human wisdom, but in demonstration of the Spirit and of
> power, that your faith should not be in the wisdom of men
> but in the power of God.

Our faith rests in a God who shakes the earth, rattles our concepts, and confounds human understanding. The power of God uproots our theology and changes water to wine. We didn't sign up for just a good bedtime story. We signed up for Jesus, and when we have Jesus, we have the Kingdom. That includes all the stories we read in Scripture, plus a host of miracles we can't even imagine—greater things than these (John 14:12).

If the goal is to be Kingdom-minded, we need to think, eat, sleep, and breathe Jesus—but not in a religious way. The goal is not to look religious or to conform to some Christian standard. The answer is not a formula, nor is it rule keeping. The simple answer is, always, relationship with Jesus. We can invite Him to be so much a part of our lives that our thoughts come to mirror His, and we literally become *Kingdom-minded.*

For steps to increase the Kingdom of God in your life, turn to the appendix at the back of this book.

CONTEMPLATIONS

God is eternally invested in you!
When you change the way you see you,
that partnership begins paying dividends.
What is a first step toward seeing yourself as God sees you?

If you focus on God, you make room for God in your life.
If you focus on Scripture, you make room
for the truths of Scripture in your life.
Do you have a signature Scripture that defines
who you want to be in the Kingdom?

Chapter 10

THE GOD WHO WAITS

How to Increase Your Authority

Therefore, the LORD will wait, that He may be gracious to you; and therefore He will be exalted, that He may have mercy on you. For the LORD is a God of justice; blessed are all those who wait for Him.

— ISAIAH 30:18

Why is it that God doesn't always move in a clear way that displays His glory?

As things often are in the spirit realm, the answer is both simple and complex: He is waiting for us. We think we are waiting for Him to move, but He is waiting for us. Many of us know how to wait for God, but we don't always take Isaiah 30:18 to heart. God wants to be gracious to us, so He is waiting. He is waiting for us to "seek first the Kingdom of God and His righteousness, and all these things shall be added to you" (Matthew 6:33).

- He is waiting for us to think Kingdom thoughts.

- He is waiting for us to have Kingdom faith.

- He is waiting for us to expect Him to be active in our lives, so we can fulfill the Great Commandment to bear fruit and subdue the earth.

- He is waiting for us to cry out for His Kingdom to come on earth as it is in Heaven.

- He is waiting for us to *expect* that He is still God and He has never changed.

- He is waiting for us to change our thinking.

- He is waiting for us to believe that He can *reconceive* and truly transform our hearts.

- He is waiting for us to believe that our thoughts can be made new in a moment.

- He is waiting for us to understand that we make choices and then *those choices make us.*

- He is waiting for us to understand that our choices determine our attitudes about life, which determines the lens through which we see the world.

He is waiting for us to understand that a tainted lens will always produce a tainted perspective, no matter how clear the object might be. Jesus is a very clear "object," but if we have a tainted lens, we will not be able to see Him for who He is. We won't be able to see everything He provided for us.

Our thoughts and choices are made by the books we choose to read, the shows we choose to watch, the people we choose to listen to, and the thoughts we choose to tolerate and allow to linger in our minds. Those things will make our choices for us, because we make choices from our thoughts, and we choose what goes inside us.

The choice of righteousness will always result in more of the Kingdom in our lives. Any time we choose Jesus, any time we stop what we are doing and turn our thoughts toward Him, any time we glance in His direction—it will always result in more of the Kingdom in our lives. We have a God who is so great . . . yet how we think can limit Him to small things!

AUTHORITY WINS OVER POWER

Satan is called the god of this age (2 Corinthians 4:4), but he didn't have that position when he first arrived on the earth. He was a fallen angel, a being cast out of Heaven, and the only way he could gain the authority he craved was by seducing Adam and Eve in the garden. With the Fall in the garden, humanity gave Satan the authority that made him a god. When Adam and Eve chose to obey him instead of God, they took off the mantle of their God-given authority and handed it to the enemy.

We still yield that authority to the devil today, but it happens individually, based on our choices and actions. Anything we have in common with Satan is the degree we have yielded authority to him. Some people argue that point and say, "God's grace covers my sin." Yes, we are saved by grace. There is no lack in the grace of God; His grace covers us completely, and He gives us something we are not worthy of: His mercy. It is the blood of Jesus that takes away sin, and because of this, He forgives us when we repent. At salvation we were given an initial measure of spiritual authority—yet His grace does not keep our authority intact, and sin diminishes our authority. As long as we fail to understand that reality, the church will become increasingly powerless as we wait for power.

In John 14:30, Jesus told His disciples, "I will no longer talk much with you, for the ruler of this world is coming, and he has nothing in Me." In other words, He told them, "I've never yielded to him. He has no hook in Me. He has nothing that ties Me to him." The enemy had nothing in common with Jesus. What do we have in common with the enemy? To the degree of that commonality is the degree we lack spiritual authority. The only way Satan has ever been able to oppress, dominate, or cause problems in our lives is because we have given him our authority at some level.

A disconnect exists between the power we are waiting for and the authority we don't have. Without authority, power is like a firecracker—a brief flare of light. But with authority, power is like a stick of dynamite that can cause extreme, permanent change in its environment. When power meets power, there is merely a clash, but when authority and power meet power, authority wins. Power is recognized when it is exerted, but true authority is recognized before anything happens.

As Jesus approached, demons cried out, "What have we to do with You, Jesus, You Son of God? Have You come to torment us before the time?" (Matthew 8:29). Demons recognize authority. They knew that Jesus had authority before He made a move against them, yet His power was recognized only after He acted; therefore, authority precedes power, and authority is greater than power.

***

THE REINTRODUCTION

As we spend time with God, we come to understand obedience, because no one can spend a long time with God without obeying Him. Obedience can be a difficult subject for some of us, but when we understand that it originates in intimacy, we begin to see ourselves as children, not as slaves.

When God asks us to do something and we say, "No," how does that draw us closer to His throne? Instead, it causes us to take a step back, away from Him, and five or ten years later we wonder why we aren't different. Or we look at our lives after a revival or a deep encounter with the Lord and think, *I'm not even as close to God as I was then. Why am I worse off now?*

We serve a God who promises that no one who comes to Him will ever be turned away. He says there is no condemnation for those who belong to Him and who walk according to His Spirit (Romans 8:1). In Jesus' famous parable in Luke 15, God is the good Father who saw His broken, dirty, repentant son walking up the road and ran to meet him. God is good, more than we could ever imagine. And because He is good, He does not want us to have anything to do with darkness, which brings ultimate decay and destruction.

If we don't keep our eyes on the main point—relationship with God—it is possible to talk about obedience and build a case for religion. But we don't obey God because we are good rule-keepers. We obey God because we want Him. He is our choice, and, as we have discussed since page 1 of this book, the choices we make in life are important.

I think that in the coming season, the Church as a whole is going to be reintroduced to the Father, and a hunger for authority will follow. With that hunger for authority, we are going to have more spiritual encounters than we have had in over one hundred years. That hunger for God's authority, combined with power, is where true signs and wonders take place. We are going to take on a heart of obedience, which is the heart of a servant. And we are going to take on a heart of submission, which is the heart of a friend.

CONTEMPLATIONS

We often believe we're waiting on God,
when He's actually waiting on us.
Have you been waiting on the Lord to act
in a particular area of your life?
Could it be that He is waiting for you to change your perspective
or to see your circumstances from a Kingdom mind-set?

Communion (two-way communication) with God
renews our minds and transforms our hearts,
but it takes a lifestyle of communion with Him to change
our soulish habits and behavior.
How do you practice communion with God personally?

Chapter 11

THE UMBRELLA PRINCIPLE

The Power of Living an Obedient Lifestyle

I think the sometimes messy and confusing concept of obedience can be better understood with a simple word picture. Obeying God is like using an umbrella on a cold, rainy day. The objective is to stay as close to the center of the umbrella as you can, because that keeps you dry. If you hold the umbrella away from you, you get rained on.

That image is an uncomplicated way to think about obedience. Every moment, we have the opportunity to make choices according to the soul or the spirit. The more soul we choose, the farther we drift from the center of the umbrella, the closer the cold rain comes, and our sleeves start to get wet. But the more spirit choices we make, the closer we move toward the center of the umbrella and the more we're protected from what we're trying to avoid. God is at the center of the umbrella. He covers us and keeps us dry. We want to live as close to the center of the umbrella as we can get.

Unfortunately, many of us assume that it is perfectly normal to live at the edge of the umbrella. "Everyone else is doing it" is a familiar cliché, and we can see that is the case. "What harm is there living at the edge of the umbrella? Look—God is still covering us."

But at the edge, we get wet. We are left wondering, "Why does this keep happening to me? Why do I experience the same things over and over again? Why do I not see more of God in my life? I don't understand." Those are the questions we ask when we are living at the edge of the umbrella. We need to draw closer to the center, where God will keep us dry.

God's hand of protection is over us. When we live in the shadow of His wings, He is justified in taking action to ward off anything that might come against us. At the center of the umbrella, our circumstances and situations line up with His perfect will. The key to living at the "center of the umbrella" is obedience.

***

SUFFERING: THE S WORD

Scripture says that Jesus became obedient by the things He suffered. There are times when the Lord will intentionally take us into situations that bring us pain, not because He wants pain, but because our obedience allows Him to give us greater authority. Obedience leads to power and authority. Jesus was fully obedient, even to the point of death:

> Though He was a Son, yet He learned obedience
> by the things which He suffered. And having been
> perfected, He became the author of eternal salvation
> to all who obey Him.
> — Hebrews 5:8–9

What "perfected" Jesus? He was perfected through suffering.

Some of us understand suffering to be a result of a lack of faith. We have a "suffering avoidance doctrine" that says, "If you're suffering, it is because you did something wrong. You aren't living at a high level of faith if you are suffering." Please don't misunderstand me. It is not that God wants us to suffer—if we ever start to believe He likes suffering, we need to turn around immediately and find where we left the path. He is a good Father, and no good father wants his child to experience suffering. However, God is *justified* in giving us greater authority when Satan causes us to suffer.

If we don't understand this issue of obedience and how suffering brings greater authority, then we aren't leaving a place for martyrdom in our paradigm. Yet when we look at Scripture, the ones who had the greatest authority were those who lost their lives and were waiting under the altar for God to move on the earth. From under the altar, they cried, "Avenge us," which we could understand to mean, "Take authority over that which is subordinate to You" (see Revelation 6:9–10).

Philippians 2:5–8 reveals Jesus' ultimate obedience, and Philippians 2:9–11 reveals the result of that obedience. When Jesus became obedient to the Father, even to the point of death, what did God do? God "highly" exalted Him and gave Him a name to which every knee would bow in Heaven and on earth and under the earth, and every tongue would confess that Jesus Christ is Lord. The title *Lord* literally means "highest authority." Jesus Christ is the highest authority to the glory of God the Father. He came to earth fully human to redeem mankind and to reveal what we are capable of walking in. With His actions, Jesus told His followers, "Watch what I do, because everything I do, you can do. I am fully human. I get everything from the Father. You, too, are fully human and, relating to the Father, can do everything I do if you have the relationship with Him that I have. And I'm going to give My life to cover you with My blood, so you can have a relationship with the Father like I have. Through My blood, you will have that relationship."

Obviously, there is nothing sadomasochistic in the Christian life; we do not *look* for suffering. We do not hope for it. However, as I said, there are times when choosing to obey God will cause us pain, and that pain has nothing to do with whether or not we did something wrong. Jesus reached this conclusion in the garden before His death: "My soul is exceedingly troubled. Father, if it is possible, take this from Me, but for this very purpose, I came into this world. Not My will, but Yours be done. I will submit to You, Father, to the point of death, even on the Cross. I will submit to You."

Submission is not submission if we want to do it. Submission occurs when we don't want to do it, yet still we say, "I will do it, because You ask it of me."

Relationship with God isn't just happenstance; neither is righteousness. Righteousness has to be sought for. We are to seek the Kingdom, and we are to seek righteousness. It is impossible to be righteous without obedience, and obedience can be difficult; it may bring some type of suffering with it—but it will also get us closer to Jesus.

And He is our choice.

CONTEMPLATIONS

We obey God out of love, not duty.
Have you ever considered obedience to be an act of love?

No good father wants his child to experience suffering.
Yet God is justified in giving us greater authority
when Satan causes us to suffer.

Are there areas of your life where "pain avoidance"
is keeping God from granting you greater authority?

Chapter 12

THE POWER OF REPENTANCE

The Effective Prayer of the Righteous

Our actions are powerful. Every action we take is an invitation for good or for evil to come into our lives. Paul put it like this in Romans 6:16:

> Do you not know that to whom you present yourselves slaves
> to obey, you are that one's slaves whom you obey, whether of
> sin leading to death, or of obedience leading to righteousness?

Our god is whatever we obey, and our obedience invites that god to have authority and rule over us. When we obey the voice of the enemy, we invite darkness. When we obey the voice of God, blessings come. It is that simple. Everything we do summons something, good or bad, into our lives.

When we give the enemy the power of our obedience, he can turn to God and say, "This nation is not following You anymore. They are now following me, which gives me the right to put my people in place in their leadership. I can put my principalities, powers, and spiritual rulers in their high places. I can bring darkness into the land, because the people no longer choose to follow You." When we disobey God, the devil has the right to our land, and whenever the enemy moves in, he brings a curse because he has been cursed by God.

However, when we obey God, He is justified in improving our situation according to His desire, goodness, and provision. He puts His angels and blessings over our land. The light moves in. The shadows begin to tremble at the presence of God, and the constraints of darkness crack and shatter, routing the enemy.

When we realize there is darkness in our land, we tend to blame the darkness and not take responsibility for our actions. "God, it's not our fault that things are the way they are—it's those principalities and powers in the high places. So if we come against them and remove them, that should set everything aright." NO!

That isn't how it works. We are still sinning, just as we were before. We are still inviting the darkness into our lives. When we violate God's protocol, we come out from under His authority and aggravate the spiritual judicial system He ordained. In fact, when we come against a principality and power, we are coming against God's judicial system because He, in His justice, has to allow that principality and power to be there.

The first step in removing principalities and powers is to take responsibility for our actions. If we want to remove the darkness that rules our land, we need to realize what gave it the right to be there in the first place. Whatever powers are over our nation, we chose those powers by the decisions we made—choices from the Tree of Life or the Tree of the Knowledge of Good and Evil. Ruling powers come with each tree.

THE BEAUTY OF REPENTANCE

One of the elemental principles of our faith is the issue of perfection (Hebrews 6:1–3). However, if we are not careful, we can misappropriate the concept of grace and never see the need for perfection.

We appropriate the death of Jesus for our sins through repentance. Perfection does not exist without repentance. The more we live a repentant lifestyle—one that is tender toward God and eager to do His will—the closer we come to God. If we don't live a repentant lifestyle, it will be very difficult for us to have authority, which is why the Church today often seems so powerless. It is also why we seldom hear sermons about sin, the need for repentance, and how to become slaves of righteousness.

Remorse says, "I got caught, and I am really sorry I got caught." True repentance says, "I am changing. I am never going to do that again." If I repent but my life does not change, I have not actually repented. I may feel remorse or regret for my actions, but if I keep doing what I did before, nothing has changed. I have not truly repented, for repentance requires change.

When we are living according to God's ways, darkness cannot possess our land—nor can it maintain the possession it gained when we were not living according to God's ways. Repentance is powerful:

For the law of the Spirit of life in Christ Jesus
has made me free from the law of sin and death.

— Romans 8:2

The Spirit of Life gives eternal life to us, and we are no longer bound by the lesser law: the law of sin and death. The law of sin and death existed until Jesus came, and when He took the keys to death, hell, and the grave, the law of sin and death was abolished. By the appropriation of Jesus' blood through repentance, our sins are washed away and we receive the Spirit of Life.

The spirit of death is very real until the Spirit of Life comes! But once the Spirit of Life comes, everything else is washed away. We are made righteous, clean, and holy in the sight of God. True repentance changes everything.

———

SANCTIFIED, HOLY, BLAMELESS

James wrote that the "effective, fervent prayer of a righteous man avails much" (James 5:16). Most of us are familiar with the verse itself, but we are less familiar with the interesting road James took to reach that specific verse.

Verse 16 begins with this statement: "Confess your trespasses to one another, and pray for one another, that you may be healed." James began with repentance and ended with righteousness. The idea is that confession leads to righteousness. The Greek word for *righteousness* literally means to be innocent, blameless, or guiltless—holy before the Lord. That is what we become when we confess. We repented of what we were doing and utilized the blood of Jesus. His blood completely covered us and makes it as if we never sinned. Our sin is thrown into the deepest parts of the sea. It is as far as the east is from the west—that far it is separated from us (Psalm 103:12).

We are made righteous through repentance, but here is the key: We have to repent in order to gain that righteousness. James wrote his epistle after Jesus' death and resurrection; therefore, part of the finished work of the cross involves the need for repentance and the appropriation of Jesus' blood to cleanse us from unrighteousness.

We can pray fervently with much passion and desperation, but for the prayer to be effective, we have to have a *baseline of righteousness*, where we appropriate the blood of Jesus over our sins and we are cleansed. Then from a position of innocence, we cry out to God and He answers.

I love what Leonard Ravenhill once told me: "When prayer becomes a cry, God begins to act." Fervent prayer is necessary, but *effective* prayer is even more necessary. I believe a fundamental component of effective prayer is innocence before God. We are innocent because we have repented or, better still, we live repentant lives.

Jesus taught us to pray, "Our Father in heaven, hallowed be Your name" (Matthew 6:9). That word *hallowed* means sanctified, holy, innocent, blameless, and without guilt. We have a God who is holy and blameless in every single way. He is able to cover our sins because He Himself is blameless. A god who is full of sin couldn't cover our sins. Jesus is the only way, and so we pray and we ask the Father, through Jesus, to cover our sins and hear our prayers, and the point is righteousness. God is faithful and just to forgive us our sins when we ask Him to, and that is not a prayer we pray only once. We continually need to ask Him to cleanse us from all unrighteousness—not because we fear for our souls, but because we want to be that much closer to Him.

Somehow in today's church culture, we have accepted the idea that we no longer need to ask for forgiveness—that our forgiveness is already complete, with our past, present, and future sins automatically covered. But that mind-set leads us to a place where we lose a righteous lifestyle and even our desire for relationship with the Father, for we think His grace covers our lack of righteousness.

As we talked about in a previous chapter, grace may cover us in one respect, but at the same time, it doesn't stop the consequences of sin. God is not mocked. Whatever we sow, we are going to reap. If we sow to the Spirit, we will reap of the Spirit; if we sow to the flesh, we will reap of the flesh (see Galatians 6:8). There are consequences to a lack of righteousness just as there are "consequences" to righteousness. When we sow to the spirit, we reap the power and authority of the spirit working in our lives.

If we want Heaven's help to live supernatural lives, if we want to live above the fray—it starts off with the appropriation of what Jesus did for us. We repent and then try to remain clean before Him, living innocent lives. We seek His Kingdom and His righteousness . . . We seek Him.

The greater the degree of repentance, the more change we will experience. If a church repents, the church will experience a greater presence of God, because the absence of sin brings the church closer to Him. It pulls them back under the umbrella, where the greater presence of God can now spread and affect the rest of the city—which can then lead to even greater repentance.

THE LAW OF THE SPIRIT OF LIFE

The Holy Spirit has many names. He is known as the Comforter, the Helper, and the Spirit of Truth. He is also known as the Spirit of Life, and as we looked at earlier in the chapter, it is the law of the Spirit of Life that sets us free from the law of sin and death. There is so much I could say about Romans 8:2, but here is the crux of it all: In Christ Jesus, there is life. Outside of Him, there is no life.

CONTEMPLATIONS

His blood completely covers us and
makes it as if we never sinned.
Do you feel a difference in your spirit after you repent?

Fervently seeking the Kingdom of God in all aspects
of our lives allows Heaven's spiritual host
to act on our behalf.
What does "seeking the Kingdom of God" mean to you personally?

Chapter 13

The War Zone

Winning the Battle for the Mind

Imagine you are in a dark room. All the windows and doors are sealed shut, and you can't see a thing. You turn in a circle, searching for even one small pinprick of light, but this is the deepest black you have ever seen. There is no light to be found.

Before the coming of Jesus, the earth was like that dark room: wrapped in complete spiritual blackness. Once in a while—on the Sabbaths when the sacrifices were made—there was a flicker of light in Israel. But only a flicker. The world was dark. It was a darkness without life.

Then Jesus came.

He is the light of the world, which means that, at His coming, the blackness covering the earth split with divine light. A literal light of spiritual dimensions dawned upon the globe:

And leaving Nazareth, He came and dwelt in Capernaum, which is by the sea, in the regions of Zebulun and Naphtali, that it might be fulfilled which was spoken by Isaiah the prophet, saying: "The land of Zebulun and the land of Naphtali, by the way of the sea, beyond the Jordan, Galilee of the Gentiles: the people who sat in darkness have seen a great light. And upon those who sat in the region and shadow of death light has dawned."

— MATTHEW 4:13–16

When Jesus was born, the darkness cracked and started to panic. Satan knew *something* had happened, and he tried to shut it down by killing every male child aged two and under. He is trying to do the same thing today—to stop a great generation from arising.

Jesus appeared, a light that will never go out. It is very real—more real, in fact, than our lives today because it is eternal in nature, not a temporal reality. The result will be that the whole earth is covered with His glory. His Kingdom rules on earth as it does in Heaven, and the "kingdoms of this world have become the kingdoms of our Lord, and of His Christ, and He shall reign forever and ever" (Revelation 11:15).

In the interim, we face a battle—an epic battle between light and dark that is mentioned more than a dozen times in Scripture. Here are but a few instances:

In Him was life, and the life was the light of men. And the light shines in the darkness, and the darkness did not comprehend it.

— JOHN 1:4–5

Then Jesus spoke to them again, saying, "I am the light of the world. He who follows Me shall not walk in darkness, but have the light of life."

— JOHN 8:12

For you were once darkness, but now you are light in the Lord. Walk as children of light.

— EPHESIANS 5:8

LINE OF CHOICE

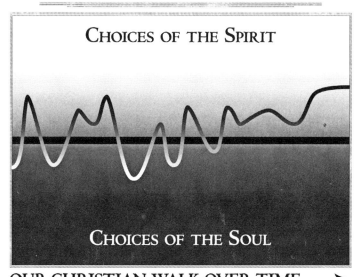

OUR CHRISTIAN WALK OVER TIME⟶

A line has been drawn between light and dark, righteous thinking and darkened thinking, between spiritual choices and soulish choices. We know that righteous thinking results in righteous choices, which result in righteous actions, which result in righteous habits, which result in righteousness, which results in destiny. As we think from the Spirit, everything starts getting better. Likewise, the moment we choose the soul and reach for fruit from the Tree of the Knowledge of Good and Evil, everything begins to get worse. Dark choices produce dark results, while spiritual choices produce results of light.

When we first start our Christian walk, we don't instantly walk above that line of choice, in the light. We don't instantly start making righteous choices. I am a grandfather now; I have been a Christian since I was five years old, and I find that I still periodically cross that line into soulish choices. But the longer we stay in Him and the more we understand His divine nature, the more we will be able to choose righteousness, because our minds contain the right thoughts.

The Lord clearly says, "Commit your works to the LORD, and your thoughts will be established" (Proverbs 16:3). We don't have to reach for an impossibly high Christian standard located far above our heads; He will actually give us the right thoughts. That is what Proverbs 16:3 means. When we seek Him, we can expect Him to give us the right thoughts, and we can trust Him in this, like little children who expect their parents to take care of them and see to their needs. Anytime we feel fear and wonder in panic, *What am I going to do?* it is a sign that we have not been thinking the right way. The presence of that fearful question tells us we haven't established a habit of thinking Kingdom thoughts in that specific area.

Instead, we should try to approach problems in this manner: *Lord, help me to change my thinking, so the next time this type of thing happens, I will be ready to handle it.* Committing our ways to the Lord does not mean we will instantly have answers to every problem we face, but it does mean we never have to hit the panic button. Quietness and confidence can be our strength (see Isaiah 30:15). We are partakers of His divine nature, and in Him is the solution to every problem. At the moment we need it, the answer will be there.

THE EMPIRE OF DARKNESS

When I was with you daily in the temple, you did not try to seize Me.
This is your hour, and the power of darkness.
— LUKE 22:53

Why is Satan called the "god of this age"? (See 2 Corinthians 4:4.) Because obedience is the highest form of worship. God even declared that obedience is greater than sacrifice (see 1 Samuel 15:22). If our obedience to God is worship, obedience to darkness must be a form of worship as well.

Just as there is a "here now" and "not yet" of the Kingdom (1 Corinthians 13:9–12), there is a "here now" and "not yet" of darkness, because there is a counterfeit for everything in the Kingdom. For everything God creates that is holy, the devil makes an imitation that is unholy. Satan rules from the Tree of the Knowledge of Good and Evil. People obey him through unbridled passions, human intellect, schemes, gossip, slander, and so forth. Murmuring, complaining, and judging reside in the world of darkness. These are effectively Satan's counterfeit to the fruit of the Spirit. "There," James says, dwells "every evil thing" (James 3:16).

Satan's dark empire has power but only within its own ranks . . . and where we have given it authority in our lives:

> But even if our gospel is veiled, it is veiled to those who are perishing, whose minds the god of this age has blinded, who do not believe, lest the light of the gospel of the glory of Christ, who is the image of God, should shine on them.
>
> — 2 CORINTHIANS 4:3–4

Satan can blind the eyes of those who desire to follow him; it is not just that they made the choice to follow him, but their eyes are literally blinded to the light. That is why it is often more difficult for a ninety-year-old to become a Christian than a five-year-old. It is not that salvation itself is harder, for salvation is simply God's forgiveness. But what is hard is the change that must happen in the mind—asking God to forgive and believing that He will act. That is hard. The more time we spend in darkness, the harder it becomes to trust God because the "cataracts" or scales that cover our eyes have grown so thick.

Psalms describes a level of darkness that is truly tragic:

> The wicked in his proud countenance does not seek God;
> God is in none of his thoughts.
> — Psalm 10:4

We can reach a place of such deep darkness that God never enters our thoughts. We never think about Him. We never consider His ways. Nothing within us is born of His light.

Without the Holy Spirit drawing us, we will always be blind. I think one of the most grievous verses in Scripture is Proverbs 4:19: "The way of the wicked is like darkness; they don't know what makes them stumble." When we walk in darkness, we trip and fall headlong, and we have no clue what tripped us up. "I can't get out of this! This has always happened to me and my family. It was this way with my parents, and it is this way with me, and there's nothing I can do about it." The darkness can encompass a single, particular issue or it can envelop our whole lives.

In Him was life, and the life was the light of men.
And the light shines in the darkness, and the
darkness did not comprehend it.

— John 1:4–5

The darkness did not comprehend the light. Those living in darkness did not have the ability to think rightly about the light and what that light meant to them. They had a history of making wrong choices, and their thinking got darker and darker.

According to Strong's Concordance, the word *darkness* means a thick black mist, like a cloud. Have you ever driven into a fog bank and had to slow down because you couldn't see what was ahead of you? Once when I was living in California, the news broadcast said that there was a 175-car pileup on I-5. Nearly two hundred cars had driven into a fog bank so thick that they couldn't see what was ahead of them. Many in the world today can't comprehend the light of Jesus and have no idea what awaits them on the road ahead.

Jesus said that having darkened perceptions leads a person to even darker perceptions. The darkness gets deeper and deeper:

> The lamp of the body is the eye. If therefore your eye is good, your whole body will be full of light. But if your eye is bad, your whole body will be full of darkness. If therefore the light that is in you is darkness, how great is that darkness!
>
> — MATTHEW 6:22–23

We can have a "dark light" within us, almost like the red light in a photography studio. It allows us to see what is going on in some detail, yet it isn't a bright light. It allows us to function in darkness, but it's still a counterfeit of the One, True Light.

THE DRAWING OF LIGHT

Just as we can have a portion of the Kingdom of God now on earth and the fullness of it in the age to come, we can have a portion of darkness now and the fullness of it in the age to come. Jesus explains this principle in Matthew 25:29–30:

> For to everyone who has, more will be given, and he will have [an] abundance; but from him who does not have, even what he has will be taken away. And cast the unprofitable servant into the outer darkness. There will be weeping and gnashing of teeth.

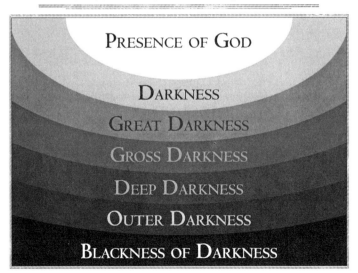

When people start making wrong choices, they end up wailing and gnashing their teeth. "What's going on in my life? Why is it like this?" Darkness always produces a corresponding pain. The deeper the darkness, the deeper the pain. It is residual pain—a day-to-day, wake-up-in-the-morning pain. It is an aching heart.

What would happen if you woke up every day to an aching heart? When we walk in darkness, we feel no hope because our hearts are sick. We lose our desire and willpower. The more we find ourselves in the deeper, baser levels of darkness, the greater the hordes of darkness can act against us on a daily basis.

What is the answer? The Holy Spirit's drawing. No one can come to the Father without Him. When we meet Jesus, we start to form thoughts that are closer to the light of God—closer to what He is doing. But at the beginning of the transition, we find ourselves fluctuating. We talked earlier about the pendulum—we go back and forth, up and down. In the moment of choice, we sometimes make great choices that are full of the light of God, and at other times, we make pretty dumb choices that are full of darkness.

But slowly, we find ourselves sinking into darkness less and less. The more we come into a place where we consistently make choices of light, the less "roller coaster" our Christianity will be. The Lord said in Isaiah 40:4, "Every valley shall be raised up, and every mountain shall be brought down" (NIV). This occurs as we make a habit of walking in the light. We can get off the roller coaster and walk into a consistent, active, full-of-faith understanding that God will be with us, no matter our circumstances.

Jesus is the light of the world. It is not just a poetic saying or a metaphor to bring us comfort and make us feel good when our lives seem dark and the way is difficult. It is reality for me, and it is reality for you. He is the light of the world. He is what we need.

Contemplations

When Jesus came,
a literal light of spiritual dimensions dawned upon the globe.
Do you notice a difference in the spiritual light
from one place to the next?

Those who dwell "in the darkness" have aching hearts
that need to see the light.
How are you going to reveal the light of God today?

Chapter 14

THE GOD WHO ACTS

Expecting the Kingdom to Move on Your Behalf

But as it is written:

> Eye has not seen, nor ear heard, Nor have entered into the heart of man The things which God has prepared for those who love Him. But God has revealed them to us through His Spirit. For the Spirit searches all things, yes, the deep things of God.
>
> — 1 CORINTHIANS 2:9–10

Several years ago a woman came up to me in the Pittsburgh airport and grabbed my arm.

"Can I talk to you?" she asked. Pulling me aside, she said, "Don't you know that you are severely limited with your gift in Christianity?"

I was caught off guard. *What?* I had never seen this woman before in my life. But then I began to register what she was talking about, and

I replied, "You don't understand. I'm not the one who is limited here. I serve the Guy who made the guy you serve. By definition, creation cannot be greater than the Creator. Therefore, I am not limited—you are."

She shook her head angrily and stomped off, muttering something like, "You Christians are all the same!"

All of us are maturing and growing to be more like Jesus, but even in that growth and maturation process, we are not the ones who are limited. As I mentioned in an earlier chapter, the only people on the face of the earth who can *possibly* have renewed, transformed, or truly enlightened minds are Christians—we are the only ones who have full access to the True Light.

The wise men and women of the world do not have enlightened minds; they have soulish minds. They might have climbed higher on the Tree of Knowledge of Good and Evil than other people, but they still climbed the wrong tree. In accordance with its name, the tree of the world offers knowledge. You can learn information about good and evil—but it is still the wrong tree.

That being said, not everything the world offers is false or untrue. There are elements in the New Age, and even in the occult, that are true—that is, they are factual, working concepts in the spiritual realm, yet they are not of God. The Bible says twice in the book of Proverbs that there is a way that seems right to a man, "but its end is the way to death" (ESV). Why choose something that is merely "good" when you could have what is truly great?

Remember, the Tree of Knowledge of Good and Evil was not just a tree of the knowledge of evil. It was also a tree of the knowledge of *worldly good.* The end result of both evil and worldly good will destroy us if we try to use it to advance our thinking over God's.

It isn't of benefit to think on things that are only "good." We are to think on things that are actually from God (see Philippians 4:8). There is a difference! Not all things that are good are from God, and there is a good that can obliterate us. All the people who have climbed high on the wrong tree can talk the talk really well, but they do not believe Jesus Christ is the only way to God. We need to climb the right tree. The Spirit knows all things, and the Tree of Life is the tree of the Spirit.

The world is familiar with the intellectual quotient (a person's IQ), but we need to pay a lot more attention to the *spiritual quotient*, because God seeks people to worship Him in Spirit and in truth. We are not on our own in this world, struggling to understand what is going on around us; we have the mind of Christ (see 1 Corinthians 2:16), which gives us the ability to understand what Scripture is saying. The mind of Christ supersedes intellect. It even allows us to understand the very issues of creation, because it is the mind of the Creator, which brings true spiritual understanding. Through the Spirit we can know all things from the One who created all things. As believers in Jesus, we are unlimited in what we can know and understand, while the world is severely limited. The enemy will fight tooth and nail to keep us from understanding that we are without limits.

If we are living righteous lives, the only thing that can keep us from having renewed, enlightened minds is not believing we can have them.

OUR MAIN FOCUS

Unfortunately, many of us have started to believe that the world knows things we don't. In some ways, that may be true—yet it has nothing to do with the enemy's strength. It is not because the ways of the enemy are somehow greater than the ways of God. It has become true for us simply because we believe it is true. We focused on a lie, and by focusing on it, we gave the lie authority and power in our lives. We believe the lie and then leave room for it to take place.

We have to change the way we view what God is doing within us, as well as the way we perceive what is going on in our lives. Again, right thinking (thinking that is based on God) will result in righteous choices, and righteous choices allow Heaven to act on our behalf. The armies of God line up on the hill, ready to do His bidding, as it was in 2 Kings 6. Elisha did not ask the angels to attack the Syrian army. He asked God, and God gave the command: "Do it." The armies of the world had nothing on the power of God. If Elisha had been focused on the enemy in that moment, he would have missed the incredible opportunity God gave him to see the Kingdom come in power.

In all things, the Kingdom of God needs to be our main focus. Anytime anything happens to us, good or bad, we should perceive it in light of the Kingdom. We need to get in the habit of asking ourselves, "What is this to the Kingdom? How is this going to advance or glorify the Kingdom?" It looked pretty bad for Elisha and his servant. In fact, from the world's perspective, it looked like they were dead. The bad guys didn't need ten thousand men to kill Elisha; they didn't even need a hundred men—one well-placed arrow would have done the trick. Sometimes, it can feel like we are in similar situations. We are completely overwhelmed and outnumbered, and it seems like we don't stand a chance.

But here is what we need to understand: No matter what we encounter, if we are righteous before God, He will act on our behalf. Righteousness is not a distant, hard-to-reach spiritual condition. It is simple. That is the great, mind-blowing benefit of asking for forgiveness—it allows us to be righteous before Him. Repentance results in righteousness, and it is as if we never sinned. His blood cleanses us from all unrighteousness, and when we are cleansed from all unrighteousness, the righteousness of Christ has come upon us (see 2 Corinthians 5:21).

The Kingdom of God should govern our thoughts, so we can accurately perceive what is going on in our lives when the enemy afflicts us. Fervently seeking the Kingdom allows all the spiritual agents of Heaven to act in our lives.

THE THRONE OF GOD

The Lord reigns;
Let the earth rejoice;
Let the multitude of isles be glad!

Clouds and darkness surround Him;
Righteousness and justice are the foundation of His throne.

— Psalm 97:1–2

The foundation of the Kingdom is righteousness and justice.

God's throne is the authority structure, the *rule*, from which all decisions concerning creation are made. That means there is no throne of God if there is no righteousness, and there is no throne of God if there is no justice. In the Kingdom, righteousness and justice must be available to you at all times. When the enemy attacks you, you are due justice.

Personally, I think that true righteousness and justice are available only to followers of Jesus. I don't mean in the court system of man but a much higher court system—the court of the Lord, the Great Judge of all creation. Righteousness and justice are available to each of us—*if* we believe it and *if* we ask. As we've been talking about, when we are righteous and clean in His sight, the Creator is justified in walking with us. He directs Heaven's agents to act on our behalf, and the world responds to our presence as that happens. We are no longer intimidated by darkness—we dispel and remove darkness merely by our presence. We walk into a dark room, and the room gets brighter. People stop us in public places and ask for prayer, because they can sense we carry what they need.

Too many times, we walk into a room full of ungodly people and find ourselves responding to the dark environment they are empowering. Enough! I've got to get out of here. I'm getting nauseated. I'm getting angry and frustrated! But they should be the ones who are impacted. Can an ungodly environment contaminate our spirits? Only if we believe it can. When we know our God and understand that "greater is He who is in us than he who is in the world," we are untouchable. (See 1 John 4:4.) No dark environment can taint us.

Unfortunately, many of us have allowed the evil one to tell us that he is mightier than he actually is. We may not say it out loud, or even think we believe it, but we act like it is true. That has to change—and it can't change until our thoughts change, and our thoughts can't change until we understand the truth of God, who He is, and just as importantly, who He is in us.

In John 16:33 we read that Jesus has overcome the world, but later in 1 John 5:4, John revealed something stunning—whoever is born of God also overcomes the world. Notice that John didn't say we will overcome or might overcome; the Word of God emphatically declares that whoever is born of God overcomes the world. That is what we do. It is who we are. We overcome.

For whatever is born of God overcomes the world.
And this is the victory that has overcome the world—our faith.

— 1 John 5:4

All God is waiting for is a change in our thinking, so we come to believe His word and forge a Kingdom partnership with Him. All of Heaven is waiting to help those who believe.

With that said, however, we do need to approach darkness with wisdom. If you are a recovering alcoholic, for example, you will want to avoid the environment of a bar, because you know where your weakness lies. Whatever your past, until God heals you completely, it would be good to avoid the slope that has been "slippery" for you. Be wise in the midst of what God is doing in your life, yet do not fear. As we begin to think correctly, we begin to live and walk in the fruit of the Spirit.

THE ENVIRONMENT OF LIGHT

Growth in intimacy and time spent with God colabor to produce righteousness and justice in our lives. Those two concepts can feel a little broad and grandiose to some people, so let's look at them in simple terms. What can righteousness and justice look like on a daily basis? They can look like these Beatitudes and the spiritual fruit of the Holy Spirit:

Blessed are the meek.
Blessed are the poor in the spirit

Blessed are those who are persecuted for righteousness' sake
Blessed are the peacemakers
Blessed are those who hunger and thirst…

— see MATTHEW 5:3–10

The fruit of the Spirit is love, joy, peace, longsuffering,
kindness, goodness, faithfulness, gentleness, self-control.

— GALATIANS 5:22-23

As we begin to understand the ways of God, we begin to live in His spiritual atmosphere. The ethos around us swirls with the activity of Heaven. We are not alone when we are called into a private meeting with our boss. We have support as we step out onto the street to do ministry in a dark, weary, pain-filled section of town. If we are righteous and clean in God's sight, He is justified in walking with us, and the fruit of the Spirit will grow to be more and more present in our lives.

CONTEMPLATIONS

Even with our shortcomings,
we are not the ones who are limited.
Are there any areas in your life where you feel you limit God?
How could you change the way you respond in those areas?

When we know our God,
the enemy cannot touch us.
What are five attributes of God that
make you feel secure and protected?

Chapter 15

THE ROCK PRINCIPLE

What Brings Life?

We lived in New Hampshire for a number of years, and we used to talk about how the land "grew rocks." Every spring when I went out to mow my lawn, I'd run over a new rock that hadn't been there a year ago. It seemed to have sprung up from the earth with the grass. In the same way, we have a tendency to "grow rocks" in our lives—we grow things we didn't know were there. It is important to be sensitive and humble enough to recognize these "rocks" as they surface. God wants to get rid of the things that keep Him from moving in our lives.

None of us are as righteous as we need to be. It isn't because we're "bad" people, that we're failing, or that we're doing a horrible job trying to live righteous lives. It is simply that "all have sinned and fall short of the glory of God" (Romans 3:23). If we want to draw closer to God and have access to Heaven's agents, God will ask us to address issues that we may have gotten away with earlier in our Christian walk. He does this to mature us, and by nature, maturity does not allow us to get away with immature things anymore. As Paul said, "When I was a child I thought as a child, and I did childish things. But now that I'm a man I have to do the things that men do" (see 1 Corinthians 13:11). God says a very similar thing to each of us: "You are in a place where I want to act, but you have to grow up. And in order for you to grow up and move forward, this issue must be addressed in your life."

Those of us with adolescent children are familiar with sitting our kids down and trying to mature their thought processes. "Listen," we say, "you need to stop doing this. Change in this area, because if you don't, it is going to keep you from walking into what God created you to be. If you keep this attitude, if you keep saying it this way, if you keep doing these types of things, you are not going to be able to keep a job. You will get fired or laid off because you haven't learned how to deal with this issue."

God wants to do amazing things for you and your family, but before He does, He wants to remove some of the rocks in the lawn. Otherwise, you'll just keep running over them and postponing the opportunities and doors He wants to open for you. That is how God moves each of us to a place where He is justified in acting on our behalf, without condoning our sin.

It may take six months, five years, or ten years to see it happen completely, but the choices we make eventually will make us. Garbage in, garbage out. Life in, life out. Spirit in, Spirit out. We get to choose.

What you focus on you make room for. That principle will play itself true time and time again. When we focus on God, His glory, and what He wants to do, we make room for His glory and what He wants to do. But if we focus on our trials and tribulations, we get trials and tribulations. In fact, they'll seem to multiply.

WHAT BRINGS LIFE?

When God allows an issue to crop up unexpectedly in our lives, it often brings pain. If it were easy to dig up all the rocks, we would have already done it! I have learned that whenever I am dealing with a "rock," my initial response can be incredibly painful, so I have to pause and ask myself, "What is the godly response He wants to surface?" I have to work through my first response to reach the godly response He wants me to have.

Arriving at a godly response requires me to think from the Tree of Life, from the Spirit of God. My initial soulish response could be, "They deserve this! Clearly, they did that to me on purpose." But that is the wrong tree. What will bring life to the other person? That is the answer I need to find. It is good to repeatedly ask through the day, "What will bring life?" That question changes everything about us. We shift from a vengeance mentality to a mercy mentality because we recognize that mercy triumphs over judgment and kindness leads to repentance.

The Tree of Knowledge of Good and Evil viciously declares, "Destroy them! They deserve it, so let's just get it over with." But the Tree of Life says, "Mercy and kindness. Respond this way, because it leads to life."

What will bring life? That question will change your entire thought process. It will change every relationship you have—not just family relationships, but as you change the way you think and begin to think according to a biblical outline, your relationships in the marketplace and church will change as well.

CONTEMPLATIONS

God brings your issues to the surface so He can mature you.
What "rocks" has God been exposing in your life recently?

When we focus on God, His glory, and what He wants to do,
we make room for His glory and what He wants to do.
Do you struggle with making difficult decisions?
Ask yourself, "What will bring *life* in this situation?"

Chapter 16

WALK IN HIS LIGHT

How to Deal with Discouragement

If you extend your soul to the hungry and satisfy the afflicted soul, then your light shall dawn in the darkness, and your darkness shall be as the noonday.

— Isaiah 58:10

When I came back to the Lord in my early twenties, I had a dream of a wheat field that was black and dead. I was standing in the middle of it, and I knew it represented my life. Discouragement swamped me as I thought, *I have no righteous seed.*

But the Lord told me, "Son, wait."

Slowly, I saw one head of wheat turn white. Then I saw another head turn white. The field was black as far as the eye could see, but as I watched, it went from complete black to dark gray to medium gray to dull white to off white to pure white.

"Be patient with yourself as I am patient with you," God said. "And if you are, this will be the result of the seed you are now going to sow."

Most of us are not good at "self-patience." We are quick to feel the sting of failure and regret, and it is easy for us to believe that we aren't growing anything of worth—the field is black.

But that is not what Jesus sees when He looks at the field.

GRACE FOR MATURITY

Sometimes when we tell people about Jesus, we end up suggesting that all their problems will disappear at the moment of salvation. But in reality, we do not become instant spiritual geniuses when we meet Him. We are governed by limitations, because we don't know how to walk with Him.

We start the Christian life with limited knowledge, limited under-standing, and limited wisdom. We don't know everything we need to know, and we usually think we know more than we actually do. We want to be full grown, but we are stumbling toddlers. We fall. We hit our heads on the coffee table and ask God to help us. "How did this happen?" we cry. "I was just trying to follow You!"

There is no shame in learning how to walk. God knows how little children operate, and no father would shame his toddler for not being able to walk perfectly. An incredible parallel exists between growing up physically and growing up spiritually. At salvation, our lives have the potential to be great, but we are still working through soul-versus-spirit issues. We call things "of God" that aren't of God and things that are of God we sometimes fail to recognize. Life is not instantly better from a maturity standpoint, but we are on the road to better. The next day will be better than the previous day. The next year will be better than the previous year—unless we start listening to what the enemy says about us and shrink back, thinking we are producing nothing but a black field.

WHERE WE ARE GOING

The path to maturity loops back on itself. We will hit the same stretch of road more than once. As we realize we have been in the situation before, most of us get sinking feelings in the pits of our stomachs and assume we must not have been successful the last time.

I'm just going around in circles. I've been here before. This must mean I'm not maturing.

But that is not necessarily true. Yes, we might have been here before—but when we were here last time, we were not as mature as we are now, and the next time we are here, we will be even more mature. We have grown. If we are not careful, the enemy can convince us that we have not grown at all. If he can do that, we will get discouraged and then we won't grow, because we will start asking, "What's the use? No matter how hard I try, nothing seems to be working!"

The key is to look at where we are and where we are going in God. This way, we will see our maturity and growth, instead of dwelling on the past.

With maturation, we don't simply go *higher* in God, we also grow broader as He flows through us, so we can touch more people. Though we start with limitations, our level of influence slowly begins to widen. We touch people and change them for the better. Others begin to see what God is doing and try to emulate us. Everything expands to a broader plane in this spiritual maturity helix as we go higher and higher in Him.

Yes, we may go over the same issues more than once, but we go over them at a higher spiritual altitude and with greater spiritual clarity. As spiritual maturity comes, we recognize that God is after the root of the issue—He wants to get rid of the rock in the lawn, remember? And so we deal with it and continue on our journey toward a deeper relationship with Him.

SAVED BY HIS LIFE

For if when we were enemies, we were reconciled to God
through the death of His Son, much more, having been
reconciled, we shall be saved by His life.

— Romans 5:10

Salvation is just the beginning. How much more will we be saved by His life?

Someone once said to me, "Jesus is no longer living! What do you mean that we shall be saved by His life?"

It is not the life He is living now, while seated at the right hand of the Father. It is the life He lived while here on earth. His life came from the way He thought, and His entire ministry was built around establishing His Father's Kingdom. "By His life we shall be saved" is tied not to our initial salvation but to our quality of life in Him.

Our lives were made to carry the same qualities as His life. It is possible to look like Him and live every day as He lived, as a "friend of sinners" (see Matthew 11:19).

The "much more" Paul talks about in Romans 5 is how we think and what we have access to. When we think and do what Jesus thought and did, we have the opportunity to walk in things the world cannot access. We have the ability to know, understand, and comprehend; we have the opportunity to make decisions at incredible speeds and depths of understanding the world cannot reach. We have access to higher wisdom, broader knowledge, and greater comprehension. These things are inherent in our life in Him. In Jesus, through Jesus, and because of Jesus, everything can be known.

When we meet Jesus, we enter into a new existence that is not governed or subject to darkness; it is governed by the light of God. We can receive the deep things of God, the things that have been hidden and unknown in the world around us. It is not because we are more intelligent, but we have understanding that transcends intelligence.

Unfortunately, much of the Church hasn't used the gifts God has given us in the way He intended those gifts to be used, because we thought it was pride. Some of us think, *The only thing I need to know about is God. I don't need to know about His creation, because this world is not my home.* Yes, it is true that we are not of this world (see John 18:36), but I don't think God meant for us to ignore or disregard the gifts He gave us that are a part of this world. The more we know what God spoke into being, the more evident His grandeur becomes to us. God is going to remove the intellectual capstone we placed on our minds, so we can understand His ways.

THE KNOWLEDGE OF JESUS

The more humanity knows about outer space and inner space, both the great things and the infinitely small things of God's creation, the more we realize there is no way this could have happened by chance. The grandeur of God in the great things and the grandeur of God in the small things are both grandeur of life-changing degree, and they prove He is here. They prove He exists and He cares for us. He is the source of all creation—the only source and the only God. The more we understand that truth, the more impassioned we will be to declare His glory. I have friends in the scientific community who tell me that the number of nonbelievers in their realm is dwindling as more and more people acknowledge that nothing but God could be creation's source.

As the blinders are removed and we see a clearer picture of who God is, Colossians 3:9–10 suddenly becomes more relevant:

> You have put off the old man with his deeds, and have put on the new man who is renewed in knowledge according to the image of Him who created him.

We could look at that verse and assume it means being renewed in knowledge about Jesus, but it doesn't stop there. It goes far beyond our current understanding because, to the fullest degree, "knowledge of Jesus" means all the knowledge Jesus has. And that, by definition, must comprise everything He created, as we briefly discussed earlier. He created all things:

> For by Him all things were created that are in heaven and that are on earth, visible and invisible, whether thrones or dominions or principalities or powers. All things were created through Him and for Him. And He is before all things, and in Him all things consist.
>
> — Colossians 1:16–17

Every aspect of the universe is intimately familiar with the fingerprints of God. Nothing that exists does so without Him. We cannot have a greater knowledge of Jesus without also having a greater knowledge of what He has done, not only in salvation but in all creation.

When we talk about being renewed in knowledge through Him, we are talking about something that gives us everything we have ever wanted and more. We have access to incredible knowledge and comprehension.

It is true that God wired each of us differently, and certain things will come to us more easily than others, but as a whole, the Church is far behind in what God wants us to know. He created us to know Him—to know His heart, to know His ways, to know His deeds. That is huge. Just look at everything He has done! We need to begin to remove our self-inflicted boundaries.

CONTEMPLATIONS

God's grace is shown in His eternal patience with us.
How are you with "self-patience"?
Are you giving yourself the grace needed to learn
from your mistakes and walk before running?

The path to spiritual maturity is not a straight line;
it often loops back on itself.
Do you ever find yourself in the middle of a "spiritual loop"?
Are you able to accept where you are on the path to maturity?

Chapter 17

The God Who Moves

Living in the Awareness of His Kingdom

For a moment, imagine that the Word of God is a cave buried deep in a mountain. Most of us venture only as far as the light falls; we are content with living near the entrance. But something happens as our eyes adjust to mystery, to the shadowed places hidden away in God—we realize there are rooms and depths and secrets we never knew existed. There are entire worlds that wait for us in Scripture. I don't know how many times I have read a familiar verse that suddenly took on new meaning for me. It staggered me and made me ask, "Why have I never seen that before?" It seemed so obvious, now that I had seen it.

It is time to leave the broad arena of the outer court behind and venture into the covered places within the sanctuary, where kings search out the secrets of the Lord (see Proverbs 25:2). Learning to feel at home among shadows and secret things requires a renewed mind, a mind that looks more like the mind of Christ than it does the mind of man.

Paul knew the importance of renewing the mind. He wanted to share deep spiritual understanding with the Corinthians and became frustrated when they were behaving like "mere men":

> I, brethren, could not speak to you as to spiritual people but as to carnal, as to babes in Christ. I fed you with milk and not with solid food; for until now you were not able to receive it, and even now you are still not able; for you are still carnal. For where there are envy, strife, and divisions among you, are you not carnal and behaving like mere men?
>
> — 1 CORINTHIANS 3:1–3

If that is what behaving like mere men looks like, what does *not* behaving like mere men look like? I am convinced that as we no longer act like "mere men," a realm of deeper understanding in the Word begins to open to us.

THE WAY JESUS THOUGHT

God the Father has always been interested in teaching His people how to think. We can see this throughout Scripture:

> You will keep him in perfect peace whose mind is stayed on you, because he trusts in you.
>
> — ISAIAH 26:3

> Jesus said to him, "You shall love the LORD your God with all your heart, with all your soul, and with all your mind."
>
> — MATTHEW 22:37

Do not fear, little flock, for it is your Father's good pleasure to give you the Kingdom.

— LUKE 12:32

The way Jesus thought had nothing to do with temporal issues. He thought in Kingdom terms and according to Kingdom timing. His mind was completely integrated with Scripture, for He is the Word; He could do nothing that was out of line with Scripture. False humility has limited the concept of the "mind of Christ" to something small and quaint that can be concealed in a tiny box. However, with the mind of Christ, we should be able to do all that He did. That means all the miracles, all the signs, all the wonders—we should be able to do even more than He did, because He went to the Father to make intercession for us (Hebrews 7:25). That was His promise.

As we read the Bible with a renewed mind, it will be like trying to capture a rainstorm with a measuring cup. We will be overwhelmed in the best of ways. "Why didn't I ever see that before? It is so clear!" The Word, Jesus Himself, will take on new shape, form, and substance in our lives, and we will know Him as we never knew Him before. We will be stunned.

The futility of the mind is not the realm assigned to us (see Ephesians 4:17–24). We have been given the Kingdom of God. We have been invited into the sanctuary. Those who enter this sanctuary realize it's much deeper than they ever anticipated. This spiritual reality drove the apostle Paul to write that God is greater than anything we could ever imagine (see Ephesians 3:20). We can spend our entire lives in a restricted world-minded paradigm—or we can embrace the mind-bending, radical, pure ways of God and become fully enlightened.

It begins with a choice.

Every one of us can live a life that oozes a deep, abiding confidence that God is really all powerful and therefore really in control of everything. This type of thinking evidences deep spirituality that can come only from the Holy Spirit of the living God. All we have to do is make the right choice. One choice at a time. And it starts with choosing Jesus.

There is no enlightened thinking outside of choosing Jesus. There is no true knowledge outside of the knowledge that comes from Him. There is no holiness, righteousness, or lasting power of any kind outside of Him.

It starts with choosing Jesus.

THE GOD WHO ACTS

In every circumstance and in every situation, whether we see it or not, the army of God is with us. We know this, because we know the ways of our God. We have seen Him and we know Him.

How many of us have a keen awareness of being surrounded by God's Kingdom authority and power everywhere we go? When we are sitting in a restaurant, are we aware of the cloud of witnesses with us? When we are at home, at work, on the highway, or in a store, are we aware of the power of God?

How many of us walk through the day knowing that the people near us will feel and be touched by the Kingdom of God? Are we aware of His presence around us to such a degree that, when we come near others, they can feel His presence on us?

When we live according to His righteousness, we can expect the invisible realm of the Kingdom to be there at our disposal. We want to become a people who know the ways of our God—we want to know what He does, and why, and how He acts on behalf of His children. We want to become a people who empower God to move on our behalf.

Believing in God at this level enables us to develop Kingdom strategies. We anticipate the enemy's ploys and recognize his deceptive practices. We understand what God wants to do through us today and so we recognize divine moments when they arrive. We respond to our friends with Kingdom understanding when they ask us for advice. We understand what is going on around us in the spiritual realm, and we lead those who follow us with the wisdom of Heaven.

Everything we need to overcome is available to us.

And it starts with choosing Jesus.

CONTEMPLATIONS

We have not been assigned to mental futility
(see Ephesians 4:17–24).

We have the mind of Christ.
In your own words, what does it mean to have the mind of Christ?

When we choose Jesus, everything begins to change.
How has knowing Jesus changed your life?

Appendix

Five Steps to Increasing the Kingdom in Your Life

Not knowing something is akin to unbelief because we can't tap into it. The unnamed servant who worked for Elisha in 2 Kings 6 didn't know the power of Heaven was there when he needed it, so he couldn't see it. It wasn't available to him, because he didn't know it was there.

Elisha, on the other hand, knew the power of Heaven was there for him, so as the servant said, "Man, we're in big trouble!" Elisha replied, "This is a great day!"

That is a remarkable difference in attitude.

We can expect the power of the Kingdom to be there when we need it. When we know who we are in God and where we are with God, we can appropriate His forces whether we physically see them or not—because we know God has sent whatever we need to overcome the enemy.

How do we increase the Kingdom in our lives? Here are a few simple steps.

1. GUARD YOUR THINKING

First and foremost, we have to guard our thinking. In 2 Corinthians 10:5, Paul tells us to take "every thought captive," and then he tells us how: by pulling down strongholds. These are issues that veil our perceptions, making us think we know what is right and wrong, light and dark, when we actually don't. Strongholds are Satan's strategy to dethrone what God wants to do and stop our purposes. If he can get us to stop pursuing our purposes in life, then we are the ones who stop our destinies. Therefore, guarding our thoughts is vital.

A foundational verse to walking with Jesus, Philippians 4:8 is more important than many of us realize. We are to think and meditate on things that are good and praiseworthy:

> Finally, brethren, whatever things are true, whatever things are noble, whatever things are just, whatever things are pure, whatever things are lovely, whatever things are of good report, if there is any virtue and if there is anything praiseworthy—meditate on these things.

Why is it important to mediate on these things? Because we become what we think and make room in our lives for what we focus on. If we focus on darkness, we make room for darkness. If we focus on God, we make room for God. If we focus on Scripture, we make room for the truths of Scripture. The Word of God will suddenly come alive to us, and we will be able to apply it in a greater way in our lives. We will start living what the Scripture says, all because we started following the principle of Philippians 4:8.

Yes, there are times when meditating on the light is difficult, but the concept itself is simple. What has God done for you that is noble? What has God done for you that is true? What has God done for you that is praiseworthy? What has God done for you that gives you hope?

As you think on these things, a change happens in the processes of your mind. You stop focusing on the negative or uncomfortable aspects of your life, and you start realizing the truth of God in you. You start doing things that are praiseworthy, so people can see what the Father is doing to help them. Your thinking takes a radical jump, and the light starts spilling out of your life in greater measure, rushing out into the shadows of the world.

2. BUILD A HISTORY OF PRIVATE VICTORIES

Second, no matter how mundane it may seem, it is good to do what God directs you to do. I have noticed that He trains me through the mundane. He and I have had several conversations that look like this:

"Pick up that piece of paper, son."

"Why? They'll vacuum the floor tonight. The vacuum cleaner will get it."

"Son, pick up the paper. It's not about picking up the paper; it's about learning obedience to Me. This is a test. Learn to hear My voice. If you obey, I will talk to you more."

When we start to obey God in the little things, we build an incredible faith that can lead to us hearing Him every day and in every facet of life. If we can hear His still, small voice, we can hear Him in the earthquake, in the fire, in the breaking rocks, and in the tornado (1 Kings 19:11–12). If we learn to hear Him in the little things, we can grow to hear Him anywhere and in any situation.

I have found that the more I listen to Him, the more I hear Him, and if I listen to Him less, He speaks less. So we need to build a history of private victories with Him—the little things no one else knows about. Did anyone see you pick up that paper and throw it away? No. No one knows that you made that phone call. No one knows you visited someone who was sick. No one knows you put money in the offering when it was hard. No one knows what you did but you and God.

This will build your confidence that, first of all, you will not fail God, and second, that God will speak to you more. You will begin to experience His voice on a more regular basis.

3. SEEK THE KINGDOM

We need to fervently seek the Kingdom of God in all aspects of our lives. As we do this, our minds will become attuned to Kingdom issues; we will have Kingdom thoughts that lead to Kingdom actions that form Kingdom habits. Once we have formed Kingdom habits, we naturally react in a divine, or righteous, way.

Righteousness can be a habit for us. The Lord loves righteous habits—when we act righteously without even thinking about it. Righteous habits are formed because we have been thinking holy thoughts, and those holy thoughts have become deeply embedded in our spirits, so much so that we now respond in the Spirit and not in the soul. Out of those habits, character comes.

4. PERSEVERE

At its core, perseverance means picking ourselves up. We keep working to build Kingdom habits; we keep thinking about righteousness and seeking first the Kingdom of God. We may fail on some points, but we succeed in others, and when we stumble we can ask ourselves, "Why did I fail? What can I learn from this? God, how can I do this better next time?" As Proverbs 24:16 says, "a righteous man may fall seven times and rise again."

Failure is a normal part of life. Yes, we will make mistakes, but we can also learn to be Christlike. We can allow God to become what He wants, and longs to be, in our lives.

Perseverance works character, or godliness, in us. Others begin to see us as people of integrity, of character. They describe us as just. They know we will not lie or cheat them. They don't have to have a written contract with us—a handshake is good enough because we've proved ourselves trustworthy.

Unfortunately, the importance of character is fading in our society, and the result is that hopelessness runs rampant. We receive hope from our character (see Romans 5:4), and that hope allows us to walk into our destinies. Without character, we have no root implanted deep within us. The birds carry away the seed that falls on the path; where the root is shallow in the stony soil, the growth doesn't last, for there is no character. We need to live in the righteous arena of good soil, where we can grow our roots deep in God and match our character to His.

5. TRUST GOD TO DO THE REST

As we commit our ways to God, He will establish our thoughts (see Proverbs 16:3). In other words, He will give us what we need. On our own strength, it would be impossible to make the necessary changes, but God is quite good at making impossible things seem as easy as a snap of His fingers. He will make up the difference in our lives, if He is justified in doing so.

In Mark 9:23–25, a father brought his demon-possessed son to Jesus. The demon would try to throw the boy into water or fire to kill him. Jesus called the generation unbelieving, and the father replied, "Lord, I believe. Help my unbelief!" The father recognized that he could go only so far. God will fill in the "holes" in our lives; He will close the gap for us and do what we cannot do. We just need to put ourselves into a place where He can act—a place where we long for righteousness and character, where we form righteous habits, take godly actions, and think according to His Word. As we do these things, God will act on our behalf and do what we cannot.

For you were once darkness, but now you are light in the Lord. Walk as children of light.

— Ephesians 5:8

About the Author

Recognized as a minister who revealed God, awakened dreams, and led people closer to Jesus, John Paul Jackson (1950–2015) was an authority on biblical dream interpretation for over thirty years. He renewed passion in people of various faiths and age groups with his sincere explanations of the unexplainable mysteries of life and enabled people to relate to God and others in fresh and meaningful ways.

As an inspirational author, speaker, teacher of true spirituality, and host of the television program *Dreams and Mysteries*, John Paul enlightened hundreds of thousands of people across the world. He found satisfaction in his role as a youth mentor and advisor to church and national leaders, as well as in the promotion of the spiritual arts.

About Streams

OUR FOUNDER

John Paul Jackson dedicated his life to passionately pursuing God and His mysteries. The results were books, teachings, courses, and a ground-breaking TV program, all of which will stand the test of time as some of the most relevant and spirit-provoking Christian teaching of our day.

OUR MISSION

Streams Ministries is an equipping ministry that offers spiritual teaching and media designed to help you hear God, reveal the often overlooked ways in which God speaks, and train and empower believers at all levels of spiritual maturity to begin using their gifts to spread the truth and power of the gospel.

REVEALING GOD

Whether you're a lifelong Christian or just someone interested in starting a spiritual journey of discovery, change doesn't begin until God becomes real *to you*. We believe God is speaking to us all the time, but some of us simply aren't hearing His voice. Our training, resources, and TV and film projects are focused on revealing the awe and supernatural presence of God to every generation.

AWAKENING DREAMS

Once you discover God is real and present in your everyday life, you'll also realize He has a unique plan on earth just for you. Our desire is to call forth that unique destiny by helping you align the dreams and aspirations of your heart with the Creator who put them there. We then offer practical training to help you reach the purpose for which you were created.

CHANGING LIVES

We aren't interested in just changing your life; our vision and goal are to train and inspire you to change the lives of everyone you meet. All of our TV, film, media, and training are designed to reach a world that doesn't know Jesus. Our training is evangelism focused, and our TV and media are created in a way to be thought-provoking to longtime Christians, as well as compelling to those who don't consider themselves followers of Jesus.

To learn more about the resources and online courses we offer from John Paul Jackson and others, please visit our website at streams-ministries.com or call us at 1.888.441.8080.

About Daystar

DAYST★R

Daystar Television Network is an award-winning, faith-based network dedicated to spreading the gospel twenty-four hours a day, seven days a week, all around the globe, on all available media formats.

Through the faithful support of partners from around the world, Daystar broadcasts life-changing programming that speaks to the spiritual needs of the global community and works to show the love of Christ to the hurting through various ministry projects at home and abroad. Such projects have included assisting Holcaust survivors in Israel with housing and medical needs, helping rescue young girls at risk of being trafficked in India and Eastern Europe, giving orphans access to education in Central Africa, bringing the Gospel to prisoners throughout the State of Texas, and much more!

Through a multifaceted platform approach, Daystar goes beyond just television, not only utilizing broadcast high definition but also mobile outlets and the Internet to take the gospel to the nations. And as a leader in Christian broadcasting, Daystar continues to raise the bar of excellence, earning multiple awards and honors, including several daytime Emmy nominations.

With a potential viewing audience of over two billion people worldwide, Daystar is taking faith-based programming into more new territory every day, but what remains at the heart of its mission is a desire to impact lives. That's why Daystar continues to offer a unique prayer service.

Featuring Prayer Partners that speak twenty of the world's top languages, anyone can call 1-800-329-0029 toll-free in the U.S. to receive prayer. Requests for prayer may also be submitted online at www.daystar.com/prayer.

For international options, visit Daystar.com for more information.